Microsoft®
Office Outlook
2003

Shelley O'Hara

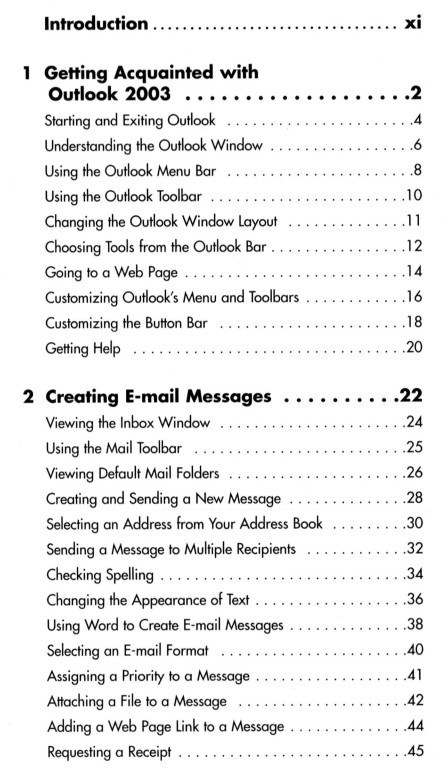

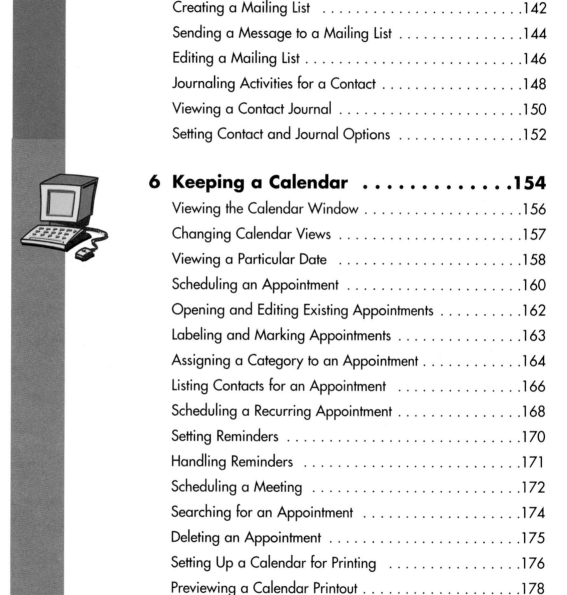

Easy Microsoft® Office Outlook® 2003

Copyright © 2004 by Que Publishing

International Standard Book Number: 0-7897-2963-6

Library of Congress Catalog Card Number: 2003103665

Printed in the United States of America

First Printing: September 2003

08   07   06   4   3   2

Bulk Sales

Que Publishing offers excellent discounts on this book when ordered in quantity for bulk purchases or special sales. For more information, please contact

U.S. Corporate and Government Sales
1-800-382-3419
corpsales@pearsontechgroup.com

For sales outside of the U.S., please contact:

International Sales
international@pearsoned.com

Trademarks

All terms mentioned in this book that are known to be trademarks or service marks have been appropriately capitalized. Que Publishing cannot attest to the accuracy of this information. Use of a term in this book should not be regarded as affecting the validity of any trademark or service mark.

Warning and Disclaimer

Every effort has been made to make this book as complete and as accurate as possible, but no warranty or fitness is implied. The information provided is on an "as is" basis.

Associate Publisher
Greg Wiegand

Acquisitions Editor
Stephanie J. McComb

Development Editor
Kate Shoup-Welsh

Managing Editor
Charlotte Clapp

Project Editor
George E. Nedeff

Copy Editor
Barbara Hacha

Indexer
Lisa Wilson

Proofreader
Tracy Donhardt

Technical Editor
Dennis Teaque

Team Coordinator
Sharry Gregory

Interior Designer
Anne Jones

Cover Designer
Anne Jones

Page Layout
Stacey Richwine-DeRome

About the Author

Shelley O'Hara is the author of well over 100 books, including several best-sellers. She has also authored business plans, a novel, Web content, marketing publications, short stories, training materials, magazine columns, a newsletter, and software manuals. She has written on topics ranging from Microsoft Windows to the International Air Transport Authority ticketing system, from Microsoft Office to buying a home. In addition to writing, O'Hara teaches training and personal development classes in Indianapolis.

Dedication

To Raymond Ball, Daddy

1934 – 2003

I will forever be "daddy's girl"

Acknowledgments

I was fortunate enough to work with an all-star team of publishing professionals, including Greg Wiegand, Associate Publisher; Stephanie McComb, Acquisitions Editor; Sharry L. Gregory, Project Coordinator; Kate Shoup-Welsh, ski racer *and* Development Editor; George Nedeff, Project Editor; Dennis Teague, Technical Editor; and Barbara Hacha, Copy Editor. Thanks also to the design team for the cool new design. It's been my pleasure.

We Want to Hear from You!

As the reader of this book, *you* are our most important critic and commentator. We value your opinion and want to know what we're doing right, what we could do better, what areas you'd like to see us publish in, and any other words of wisdom you're willing to pass our way.

As an associate publisher for Que Publishing, I welcome your comments. You can e-mail or write me directly to let me know what you did or didn't like about this book—as well as what we can do to make our books better.

Please note that I cannot help you with technical problems related to the *topic* of this book. We do have a User Services group, however, where I will forward specific technical questions related to the book.

When you write, please be sure to include this book's title and author as well as your name, e-mail address, and phone number. I will carefully review your comments and share them with the author and editors who worked on the book.

E-mail: feedback@quepublishing.com

Mail: Greg Wiegand
            Associate Publisher
            Que Publishing
            800 East 96th Street
            Indianapolis, Indiana 46240 USA

For more information about this book or another Que title, visit our Web site at www.quepublishing.com. Type the ISBN (excluding hyphens) or the title of a book in the Search field to find the page you're looking for.

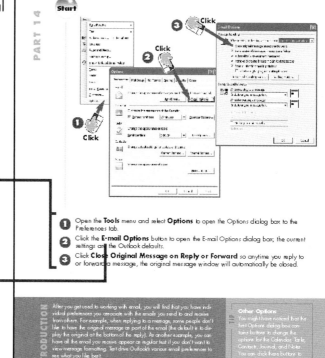

1 Each step is fully illustrated to show you how it looks onscreen.

It's as Easy as 1-2-3

Each part of this book is made up of a series of short, instructional lessons, designed to help you understand basic information that you need to get the most out of your computer hardware and software.

2 Each task includes a series of quick, easy steps designed to guide you through the procedure.

3 Items that you select or click in menus, dialog boxes, tabs, and windows are shown in **bold**.

drag

drop

How to Drag:
Point to the starting place or object. Hold down the mouse button (right or left per instructions), move the mouse to the new location, then release the button.

Introductions explain what you will learn in each task, and **Tips and Hints** give you a heads-up for any extra information you may need while working through the task.

See next page
See next page:
If you see this symbol, it means the task you're working on continues on the next page.

End
End Task:
Task is complete.

Selection:
Highlights the area onscreen discussed in the step or task.

Click:
Click the left mouse button once.

Double-click:
Click the left mouse button twice in rapid succession.

Right-click:
Click the right mouse button once.

Pointer Arrow:
Highlights an item on the screen you need to point to or focus on in the step or task.

Click & Type:
Click once where indicated and begin typing to enter your text or data.

Introduction to Outlook

Information is the backbone of most personal and business ventures, and as such, keeping track of that information is key. Think about all the pieces of information you need to manage your day. Whom do you have to call? What appointments do you have? Do you need to send some type of communication, such as an e-mail, to others? What about the communications you receive from others? Do you need to read your e-mail? What are today's to-do items?

Although each piece of information is relatively small, they quickly add up. To help you manage this flow of information, you can use Outlook. Outlook includes various program components, each useful for managing various types of information. You can use the Mail program to send and receive e-mail messages. You can use the Contacts program to keep track of contact information such as e-mail addresses, phone numbers, addresses, and more. For scheduling, use the Calendar. With this feature, you can plan appointments, meetings, and special events. In addition, you can use Outlook to manage your to-do list. For this element of your life, use the Tasks feature. And there's still more. You can use Outlook's Notes feature to jot down miscellaneous reminders. Use the Journal to track activities for contacts.

As you can see, Outlook is a full-powered personal information manager. To maximize this program and put it to use in your business or personal life, you need a book that is reliable, organized, and easy to follow. That's where *Easy Microsoft Office Outlook 2003* comes in. This book covers Outlook's most often used features in an easy-to-follow format. You can see step-by-step how to accomplish each task. The book is suitable as a how-to guide or as a reference. That is, you can read the book from start to finish, completing each task, or you can turn to particular sections of interest as needed. Either way, *Easy Microsoft Office Outlook 2003* lets you see it done and then do it yourself!

Getting Acquainted with Outlook 2003

You can use Outlook as your own personal organizer—sending and receiving e-mail, managing contact information, keeping track of appointments and to-do items, and more. All these tools are accessible from the Outlook window. To get started with this program, take some time to familiarize yourself with the layout of the window. If needed, you can change what appears so that your Outlook workspace more closely reflects your needs. You'll find information on these Outlook options in this part.

The Outlook Window

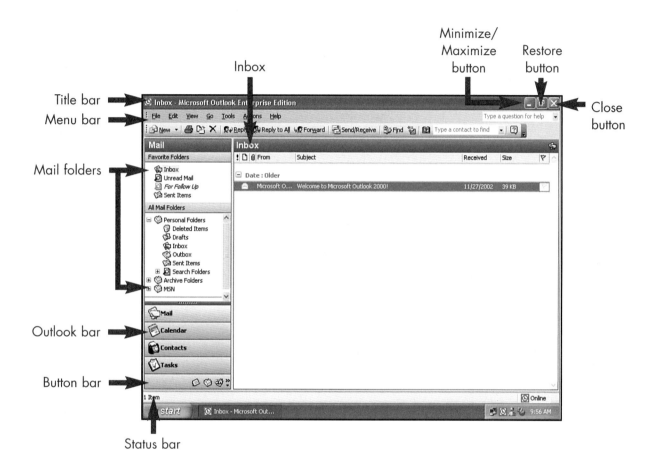

Minimize/Maximize button

Restore button

Inbox

Title bar

Menu bar

Close button

Mail folders

Outlook bar

Button bar

Status bar

PART 1

Starting and Exiting Outlook

Start

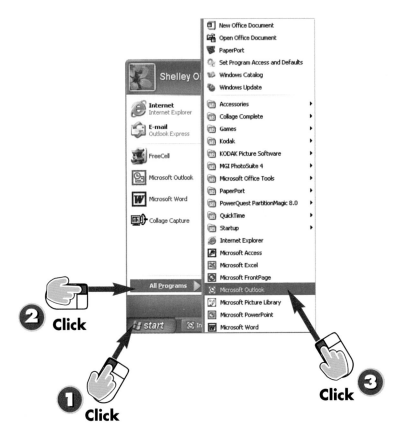

1 To start Outlook, click **Start.**

2 Click **All Programs.**

3 Click **Microsoft Outlook**.

INTRODUCTION

Outlook is a multipurpose program used to manage several types of information. You can use Outlook to send and receive e-mail, keep track of contacts and appointments, jot notes, and more. Think of it as your personal assistant. In this task, you learn how to start Outlook.

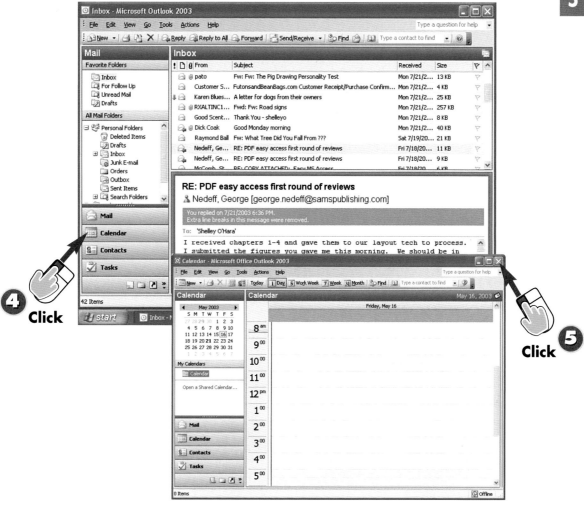

4 Click

5 Click

4 The Outlook window opens, with the Outlook Today screen displayed. To use a different Outlook tool, such as Calendar, click it in the Outlook bar.

5 That feature is displayed. To exit Outlook, click the window's **Close** button.

End

Going Directly to Your Inbox
When Outlook first opens, you see the Outlook Today screen. You can go automatically to your Inbox by clicking the **Inbox** option on that screen.

Other Start Methods
Windows XP displays your system's default mail program on the first panel of the Start menu. If you have set this to Outlook, you can click the **Start** button and select **Outlook** from the top pane of the menu that appears. In addition, if Outlook is one of your most frequently used programs, it will be listed on the bottom pane of the Start menu; you can start Outlook by clicking the program name there.

Understanding the Outlook Window

Start

① The menu bar contains the various Outlook menus that are available to you. To display a menu's commands, click the menu name. You can then click the command you want.

② Rather than selecting commands from the menu, you can use toolbar buttons to execute commands. Click the button that represents the command you want to execute.

③ The Outlook Bar on the left side of the screen is divided into several panes. The top pane(s) displays options for the tool you select in the bottom pane. For instance, if you select the Mail tool, you see Mail options.

INTRODUCTION

When you start Outlook, the Outlook window opens. It includes several panes of information as well as access to the different tools. Use this task to familiarize yourself with the various parts of the window.

TIP

Using the Toolbar
See "Using the Outlook Toolbar" later in this part for more information about using the toolbars.

4 In the bottom pane of the Outlook Bar, you click the tool you want to work with. For instance, click the **Calendar** tool to view the Calendar options.

5 You can use the buttons in the Outlook Bar to activate certain Outlook features. For instance, to display a folder list, click the **Folder List** button.

6 In the work area, you see information related to the selected tool. For instance, if you select the **Calendar** tool in the Outlook Bar, you see the current day's calendar in the work area.

7 The status bar displays information about the selected tool, such as the number of new messages.

End

Customizing the Outlook Window

If you prefer a more streamlined window, without all the options displayed, you can customize the Outlook window to display only the tools you need. Alternatively, you might choose to display additional onscreen elements so you can easily access as many tools as possible. See "Changing the Outlook Window Layout" later in this part to learn how.

Using the Outlook Menu Bar

Start

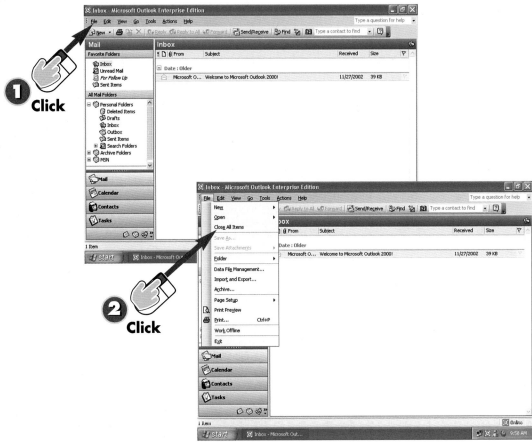

1 Click

2 Click

1 Click a menu name in the menu bar (in this case, **File**).

2 The menu opens, displaying a list of available commands. Click a command to execute it, or click outside the menu to close the menu without making a selection.

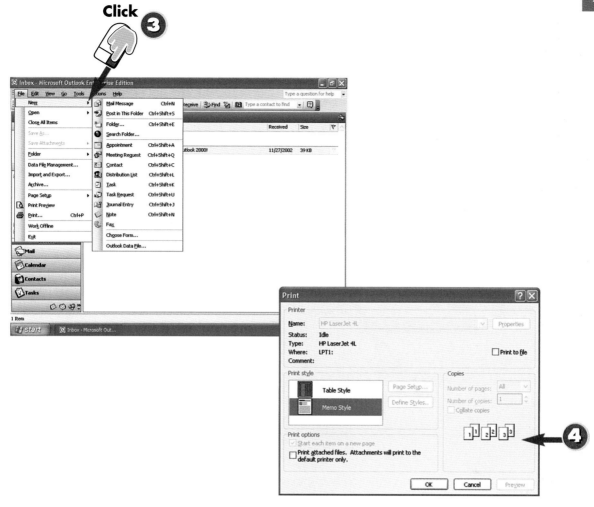

Clicking a command followed by a right-pointing arrow opens a submenu containing additional options. For example, click **New** to choose from the various new items you can create.

Clicking a command followed by an ellipsis opens a dialog box containing various options. For example, clicking **Print** opens the Print dialog box. Make your selections in the dialog box and click **OK**.

End

Expanding Menus
By default, when you click a menu name, Outlook displays a short version menu that contains only the commands you use frequently. To expand the menu to display all its commands, click the **down-arrow** button at the bottom of the menu. To configure Outlook to display the entire menu by default, open the **Tools** menu and choose **Customize**; in the dialog box that opens, click the **Options** tab, click the **Always Show Full Menus** check box to put a check mark in it, and click the **Close** button.

Using the Outlook Toolbar

Start

Click **1**

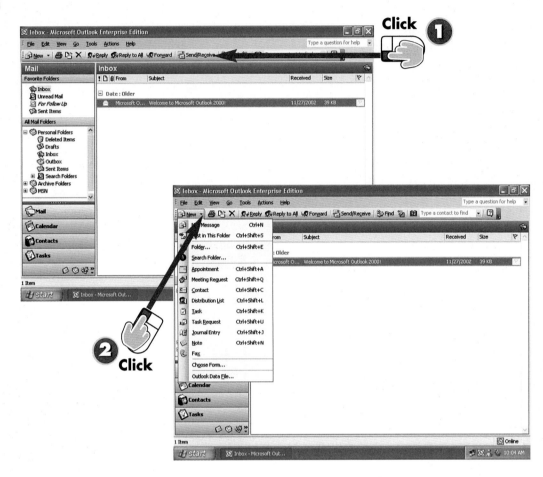

2 Click

1 Click the button that represents the command you want to execute. For example, to send and receive e-mail messages, click the **Send/Receive** button.

2 If a button features a drop-down arrow, click the **arrow** to display additional commands, and then click the desired command. For example, to create a new message, click the **New** button and select **Mail Message** from the list that appears.

End

Changing the Outlook Window Layout

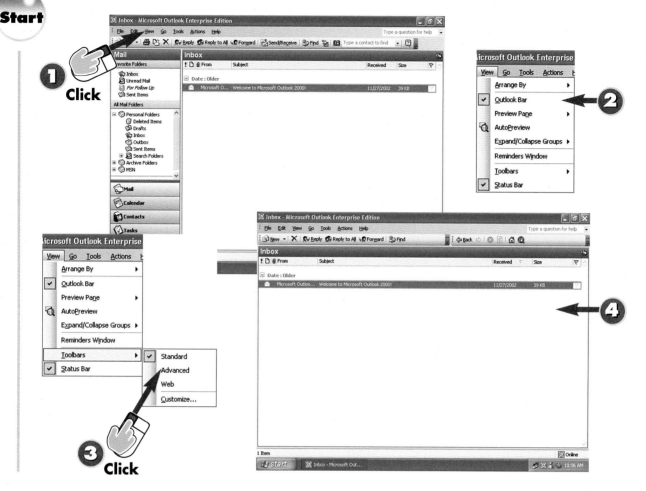

Start · Click · Click · End

1. Click the **View** menu.

2. A list of the various items you can hide or display appears. If an item is checked, it is displayed; select the checked item to hide it.

3. To hide or display toolbars, open the **View** menu and choose **Toolbars**. A submenu of available toolbars appears; select an unchecked toolbar to display it, or select a checked toolbar to hide it.

4. The change is made. Here you see the Outlook window with the Web toolbar displayed and the Outlook Bar hidden.

INTRODUCTION

If you prefer a more streamlined Outlook window, you can hide some of the toolbars and other screen elements. Alternatively, if you prefer to display more options in the Outlook window, you can display additional items onscreen.

Choosing Tools from the Outlook Bar

Start

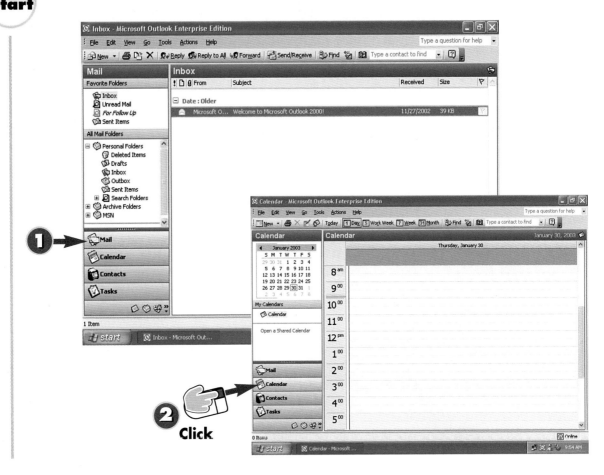

2 Click

1 The currently selected tool (in this case, **Mail**) is highlighted in the Outlook Bar. The menu, toolbar, and Outlook Bar display elements that pertain to this tool.

2 To view the calendar, click **Calendar** in the Outlook Bar. You can use Outlook's Calendar to keep track of important dates, meetings, and other scheduled events.

PART 1

INTRODUCTION

When you want to select a different Outlook tool, you do so by clicking the tool's button in the Outlook Bar. Outlook, by default, starts in Mail, but you can easily switch to Calendar, Contacts, Tasks, Notes, Folders, or Shortcuts.

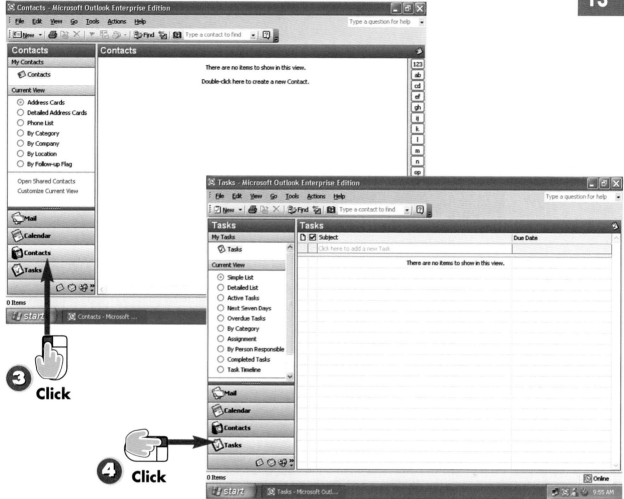

Click

Click

To view Outlook's Contacts feature, click **Contacts** in the Outlook Bar. You can use this feature to store e-mail addresses and other key information about your friends, colleagues, family members, and others.

If you need help keeping track of all the things you have to do, click the **Tasks** tool to use Outlook's task list. You use it to track dates for start and completion, as well as expenses and other information.

End

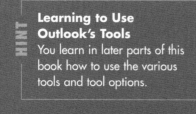

Learning to Use Outlook's Tools
You learn in later parts of this book how to use the various tools and tool options.

Going to a Web Page

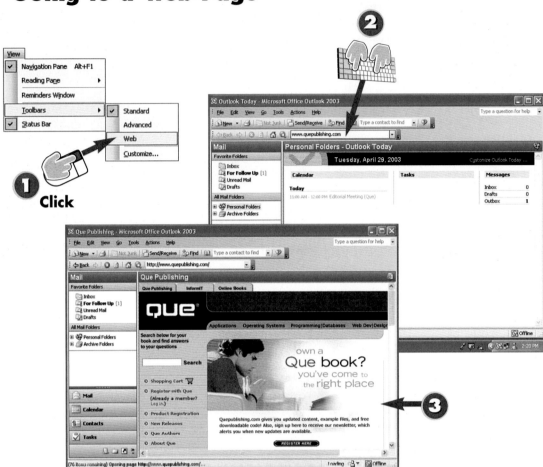

Start

Click

1. Open the **View** menu, choose **Toolbars**, and select **Web**.

2. The Web toolbar appears. Type the address of the Web page you want to visit and press **Enter**.

3. The Web page whose address you typed is displayed in the main Outlook window.

TIP

Web Addresses

Web addresses (also called *URLs*) are in this format: **www.*domain-name.ext***. You can often leave off the **www**, which stands for World Wide Web. ***domainname*** refers to the site name. (You can sometimes guess a site's domain name by typing the company or site name. For example, the domain name for the NBA's Web site is **nba**.) **ext** stands for *extension* and indicates the site's type. Common extensions are **.com** (commercial), **.net** (network), **.org** (organizations and nonprofit groups), and **.edu** (education).

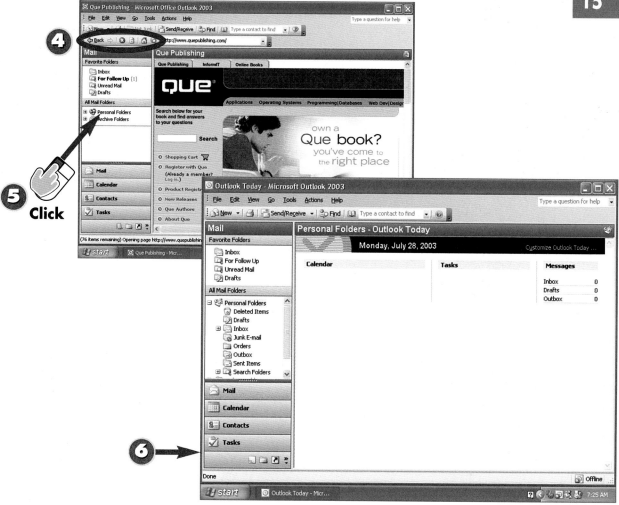

4 Use the toolbar buttons to navigate to other pages, including going back a page, going to your start page, and stopping the display of a page.

5 To close the Web site, click any of the other Outlook tools. (Be sure also to log off your Internet connection if needed.)

6 The Web page is closed and you see the view for the selected tool (here, Outlook Today).

Hiding the Toolbar
To hide the toolbar, open the **View** menu, choose **Toolbars**, and select **Web**. Doing so hides the toolbar but does not close the Web page that is displayed. You must select another Outlook feature to remove the page from the Outlook window.

Moving the Toolbar
You can move the toolbar by clicking the left-most portion of the toolbar and dragging it to the desired spot.

Customizing Outlook's Menu and Toolbars

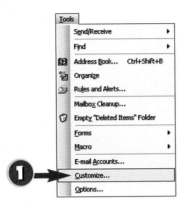

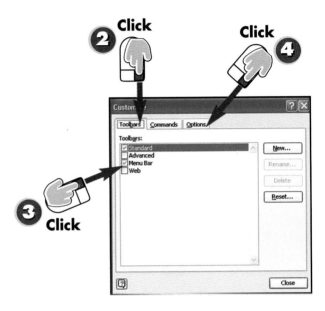

Click

Click

Click

1. Open the **Tools** menu and choose **Customize**.

2. The Customize dialog box opens. Click the **Toolbars** tab if it's not displayed already.

3. Check any toolbars that you want displayed in Outlook and uncheck any you want hidden.

4. Click the **Options** tab.

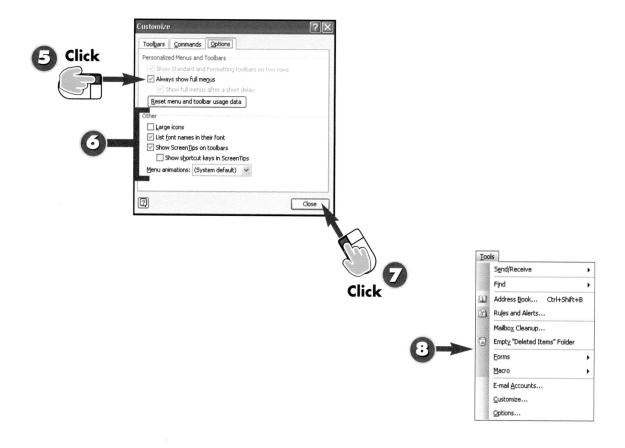

5 To configure Outlook to display only those menu commands you use most often, make sure the **Always Show Full Menus** check box is unchecked.

6 Make changes as desired to how fonts are displayed, whether ScreenTips are displayed, and whether Outlook uses menu animations.

7 Click **Close** to confirm your changes.

8 You see the effects of your changes (short menus).

End

Turning Toolbars On and Off
You can also turn toolbars on and off using View, Toolbars.

Customizing Menu Commands
Although you can customize the menu commands that are listed, it's not a great idea to do so because the online help and other materials, such as this book, reference the menus as originally created. If you do want to customize the commands, however, you do so using the **Commands** tab in the **Customize** dialog box.

Customizing the Button Bar

Start

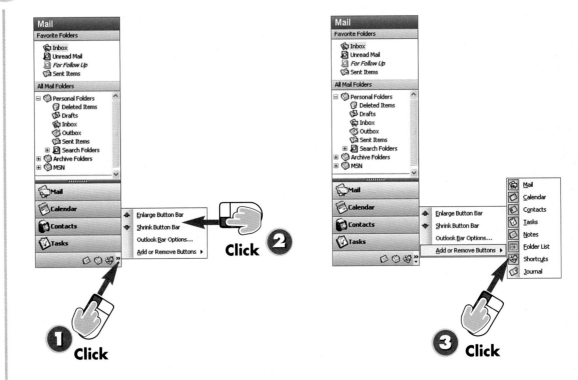

Click

Click

Click

1. Click the **Configure Buttons** arrow in the Outlook Bar to display a menu of choices.

2. To enlarge the Button Bar, click the **Enlarge Button Bar** option. To make the Button Bar smaller, click **Shrink Button Bar**.

3. To add or remove buttons from the Button Bar, click **Add or Remove Buttons** in the Configure Buttons menu. In the list that appears, click highlighted buttons to remove them or unhighlighted buttons to add them.

The Outlook Button Bar, located at the bottom of the Outlook Bar, includes several buttons that enable you to quickly access various Outlook tools. You can customize the Outlook Button Bar to make it smaller (making more room for the top panes), and you can add or remove buttons. Select a layout that makes it easy for you to access the tools you use most frequently.

TIP

Making Buttons Bigger or Smaller
You can select the **Enlarge Button Bar** and **Shrink Button Bar** commands more than once. Each time you do, the buttons in the Button Bar grow or shrink, depending on your selection.

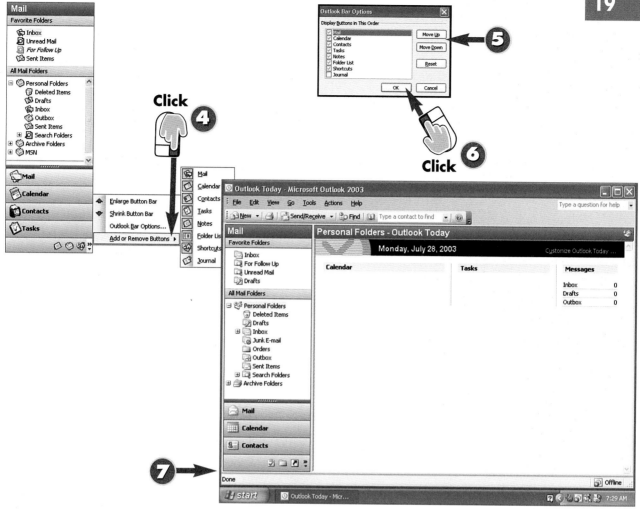

Click 4

Click 6

4️⃣ To change the order of the buttons, click **Outlook Bar Options** in the Configure Buttons menu.

5️⃣ The Outlook Bar Options dialog box opens. Select the button you want to move up and click **Move Up**. Alternatively, select the button you want to move down and click **Move Down**.

6️⃣ Click **OK** to confirm your choices.

7️⃣ You can see the effects of your changes.

End

Hiding Buttons

You can use the Outlook Bar Options dialog box to hide or display buttons. Any buttons that are checked are displayed; you can turn a button on or off by clicking the check box next to it.

Resetting Buttons

To reset the buttons to the original, default order, click **Reset** in the Outlook Bar Options dialog box.

Getting Help

Start

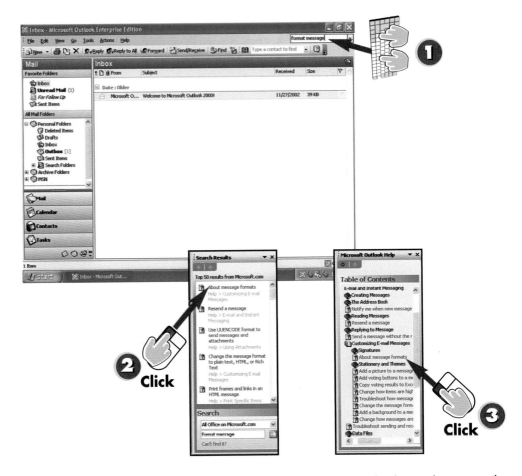

Click

Click

---

1 In the **Help** box, located in the upper-right corner of the Outlook window, type keywords for the topic or question on which you want help (in this case, **format message**), and press **Enter**.

2 The Search Results pane opens, listing help topics that match the criteria you typed. Click the topic that appears to answer your question.

3 Outlook's Help program downloads a table of contents from the Microsoft Office help site. Articles on that site that pertain to your search entry appear in blue; click one whose title matches the information you seek.

Click 6

Click 5

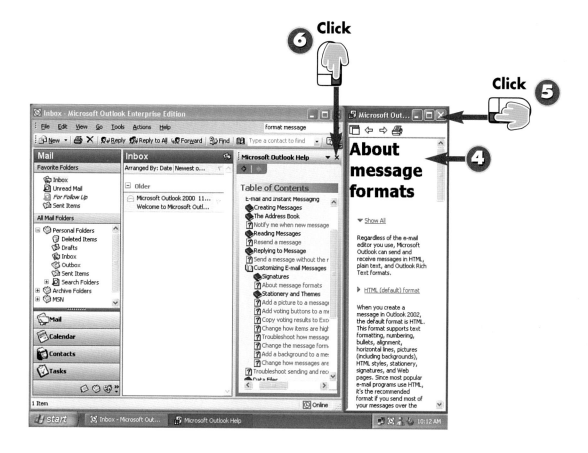

4 A window displaying the help information opens. Review this information.

5 Click the article window's **Close** button to close it.

6 Click the Search Results (now titled Microsoft Outlook Help) pane's **Close** button to close it.

End

Getting Help Offline
If you are not online, you can use Outlook's built-in help by following the steps in this task. You'll see related topics from Outlook's help files; simply click the topic of interest.

Using Other Help Options
Another way to get help is to use the Help menu. Click **Help**, **Microsoft Outlook Help**; then type a question or keyword into the text box and click the **Search** button. Alternatively, click **Table of Contents** in the Help window to browse by topic through the various help articles.

Creating E-mail Messages

The most popular tool in Outlook is the e-mail program, which you can use to send and receive e-mail messages. Outlook includes toolbar buttons and commands to make sending messages and adding elements such as a link to a Web site or a file as easy as possible. This part discusses the basics of sending mail. (Part 3, "Reading and Handling E-mail Messages," covers receiving mail, and Part 4, "Using Advanced Mail Features," covers more advanced features of the mail program.)

Creating a New E-mail Message

Send button

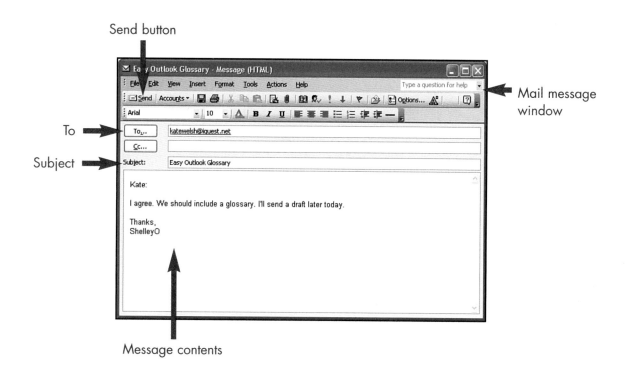

To

Subject

Mail message window

Message contents

Viewing the Inbox Window

Start

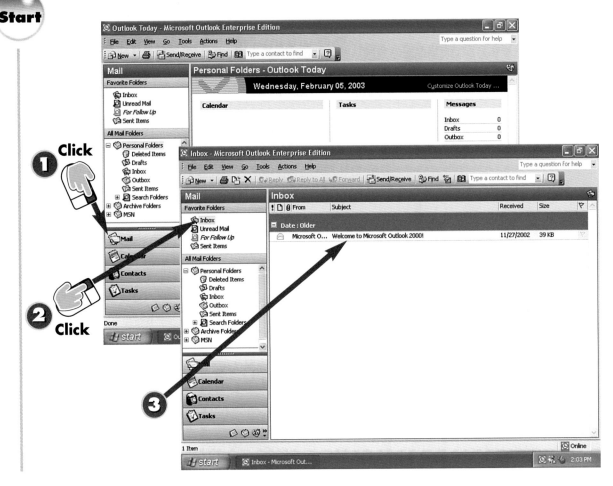

Click ①

Click ②

③

1. If needed, click the **Mail** option in the Outlook bar.

2. In the Outlook window, click **Inbox** under All Mail Folders.

3. The Inbox appears, featuring any e-mail messages you have received.

End

TIP

Displaying the Preview Pane
You can choose to display a Preview pane that displays the header and partial contents of the selected message. To do so, open the **View** menu, choose **Preview Pane**, and specify where the Preview pane should be placed. This pane may already be displayed.

Using the Mail Toolbar

Start

Click ①

Click ② ③ **Click** ④

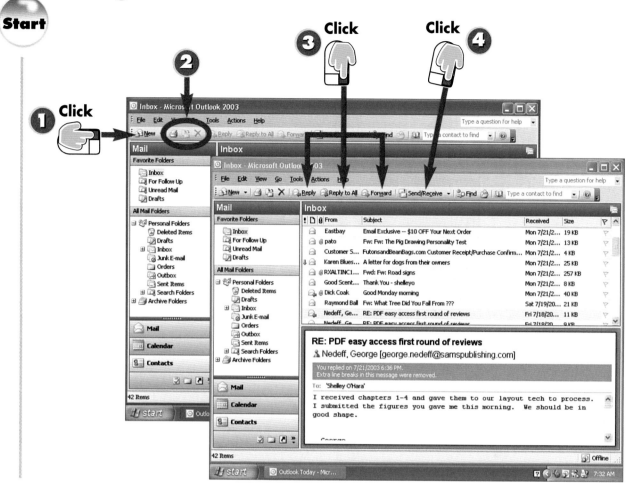

① With the Inbox displayed, click the **New** button to create a new message.

② Use the next three buttons in the toolbar to print, move, and delete messages. (You must select a message first.)

③ To reply to or forward a message, select a message and then click the **Reply**, **Reply to All**, or **Forward** button.

④ Click the **Send/Receive** button to check for new messages and to send any messages you have created.

End

INTRODUCTION

Outlook changes the menu bar and toolbar depending on which tool you are working with. When you are checking and sending messages in the Mail window, you see commands and toolbar buttons for working with messages.

TIP

Using Toolbar Buttons
Later tasks in this part and others cover using these buttons in more detail. If you are unsure what a button does, place the mouse pointer over a button; a ScreenTip appears, containing the name of the button.

Viewing Default Mail Folders

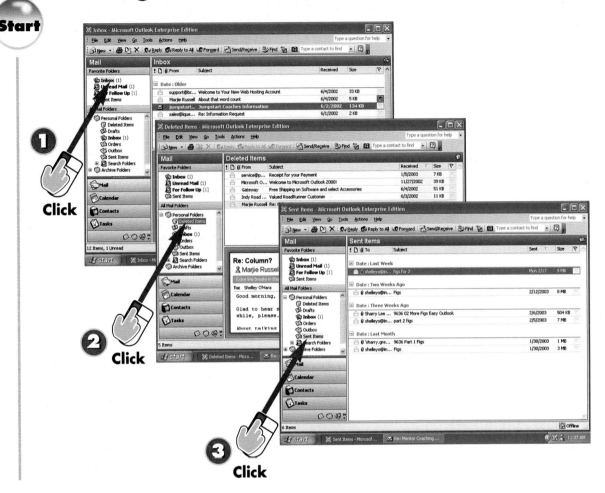

Start

1 Click

2 Click

3 Click

1 To display the contents of the Inbox, click **Inbox** under Favorite Folders or All Mail Folders. Here you see any messages you have received.

2 To view items you have deleted, click the **Deleted Items** folder. The contents of this folder are displayed.

3 To view messages you have sent, click the **Sent Items** folder. A list of the messages you have sent appears.

Outlook sets up default mail folders for common items, including the Inbox for mail you've received, the Outbox for mail that's ready to be sent, as well as Sent Items, Deleted Items, and Drafts. Outlook also automatically sets up certain Favorite Folders. You can use this folder list to quickly access commonly used folders. You can select a folder from the Favorite Folders or the All Mail Folders list to display the contents of any listed folder.

Displaying the Folder List

TIP

By default, when the Mail feature is selected, Outlook displays only mail folders in the Outlook Bar. To display all your Outlook folders—not just the ones related to Mail—in the Outlook Bar, click the **Folder List** button in the Outlook Bar.

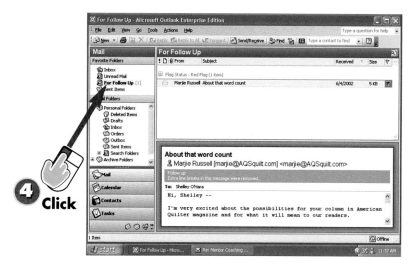

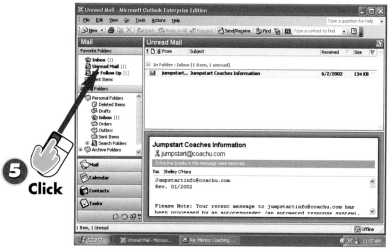

4 Click the **For Follow Up** folder in the Favorite Folders list to display any messages you have flagged for follow-up.

5 To view all unread messages, even ones you've deleted, click the **Unread Mail** folder.

End

Customizing Favorite and Folders
For information about customizing the folders in the Favorite Folders, see "Adding Folders to the Favorite Folders List" later in this part.

Creating and Sending a New Message

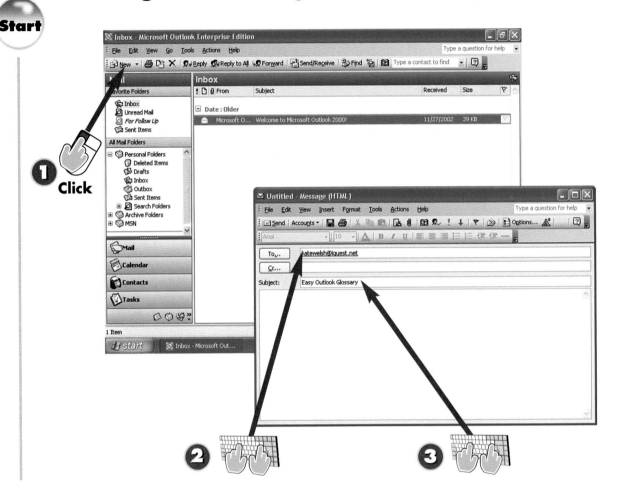

Start

1 Click

2 **3**

1 In Mail view, click the **New** button in the Outlook toolbar. An Untitled Message window opens.

2 In the **To** field, type the recipient's e-mail address. (To send the message to additional people, separate each address with a semicolon.)

3 In the **Subject** field, type a subject for the message.

INTRODUCTION

When you want to use Outlook to send a message to someone, you open a new mail message. You then enter the person's address, type a subject for the message, and type the contents of the message. This task covers the basics of creating an e-mail message; other tasks in this part provide more details, as well as other options for creating e-mail messages.

TIP

Using Alternate Programs
This book uses the Outlook mail program for creating messages. You can also use Word to create e-mail. See "Changing the Mail Program" and "Using Word to Create E-mail" in Part 4.

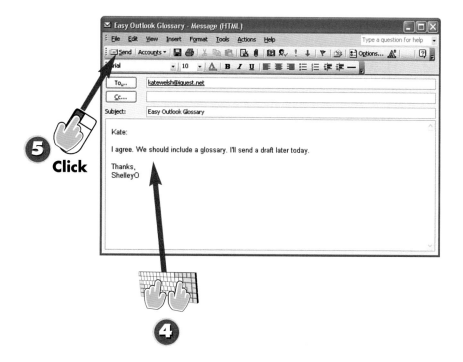

5 Click

4

4 Click in the message area and type a message.

5 Click **Send** on the Message window's toolbar. Assuming you are online and have set up Outlook to automatically send your messages, the message will be sent.

End

Typing an Address

The most important part of an e-mail message is the address. If you type the address incorrectly, your message will not be delivered. Addresses follow the format **username@domain.ext**—for example, **sohara@msn.com**. **username** refers to the person's e-mail name (**sohara**); **domain** is the name of the person's mail or Internet provider (**msn**), and **ext** is the extension and indicates the type of provider (**com**).

When Messages Are Sent

Your messages are sent immediately when you click **Send**. If you are working offline or if you have not set up for immediate delivery, the messages are stored in the Outbox until you click **Send/Receive**. See Part 4 for more information.

Selecting an Address from Your Address Book

Start

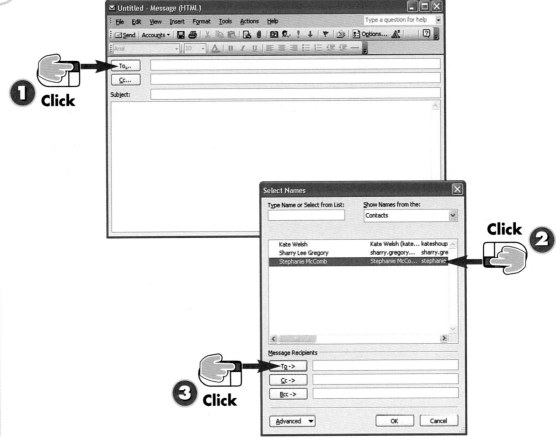

1 Click

2 Click

3 Click

1 Create a new mail message (refer to the task "Creating and Sending a New Message" for help). Then, in the Untitled Message window, click the **To** button.

2 The Select Names dialog box opens, listing all the names in your Address Book. In the list, click the name of your recipient.

3 Click the **To** button.

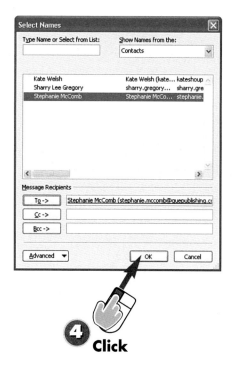

4 Click

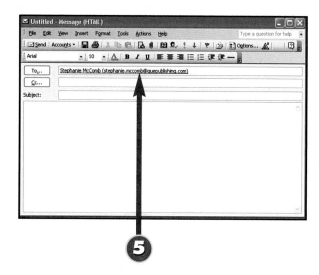

5

4 The name is added to the Message Recipients list. Click **OK**.

5 The name is added to the To box in the mail message. Type a subject for the message, type the message body, and send the message as usual.

End

Selecting a Name in the Address Book
If your Address Book contains a long list of addresses, you can quickly locate the name you want by typing the first few characters of the name. Outlook scrolls to and selects the first name that matches your input.

Sending a Message to Multiple Recipients

Start

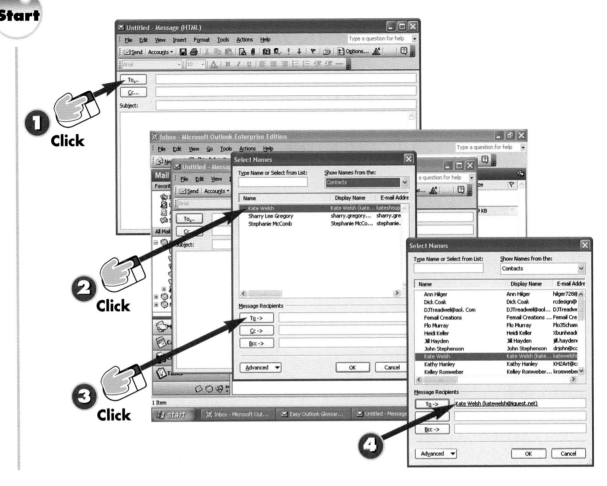

1 Click

2 Click

3 Click

4

① Create a new mail message (refer to the task "Creating and Sending a New Message" for help). Then, in the Untitled Message window, click the **To** button.

② The Select Names dialog box opens, listing all the names in your Address Book. Click the name of the first recipient in the list.

③ Click the **To** button.

④ The name is added to the Message Recipients list. Repeat steps 2 and 3 to add more names to the To list.

There will undoubtedly be times when you want to send the same message to several people. In that case, you can select several names from the To list. You can also add addresses to the Cc (carbon copy) and Bcc (blind carbon copy) fields. (When you add a name to the Bcc field, that name is not listed among the recipients of the message.) In this task, you'll learn how to use your Address Book to send a message to multiple recipients.

Typing Multiple Names
If you prefer to type names into the e-mail message's To field instead of using your Address Book, you can enter multiple recipients by separating each e-mail address with a semicolon.

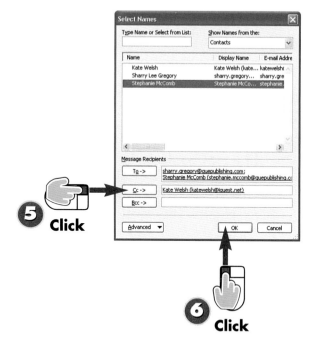

5 Click

6 Click

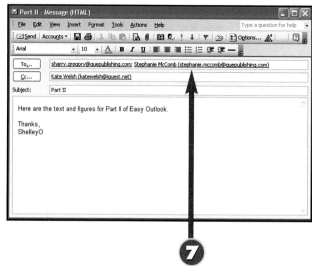

7

5 To add a name to the Cc or Bcc list, select the name and click the **Cc** or **Bcc** button.

6 When you're finished adding names to the Message Recipients list, click **OK**.

7 The names are added to the To, Cc, and/or Bcc boxes in the mail message. Type a subject for the message, type the message body, and send the message as usual.

End

Removing a Name from the Address List
To delete a name from the To, Cc, or Bcc list, click the name to select it and then press the **Delete** key on your keyboard. You should also delete any left over spaces and semicolons.

Creating a Mailing List
If you frequently send messages to the same group of people, consider setting up a mailing list for that group. That way, you won't have to enter all the names each time you send a message to the group. For more information on creating mailing lists, see Part 4.

Checking Spelling

Start

Click 2

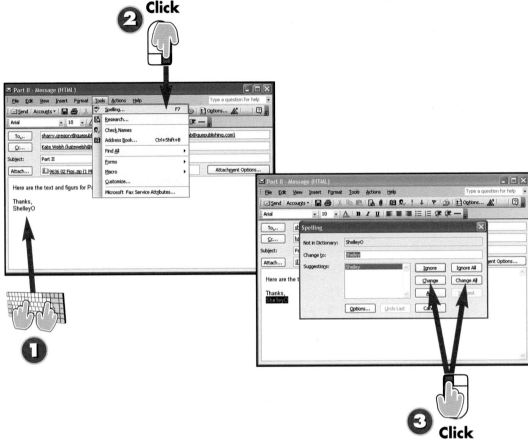

Click 3

1. Create a new message, completing the To and Subject fields and typing the message text.

2. Open the **Tools** menu and choose **Spelling** to start Outlook's Spell Checker. Outlook compares the words in your message to words in its dictionary, flagging any words it cannot find.

3. If a word that has been flagged is spelled incorrectly, and the correct spelling is listed in the Spelling dialog box, select the correct word from the Suggestions list and click **Change** or **Change All**.

Click 4

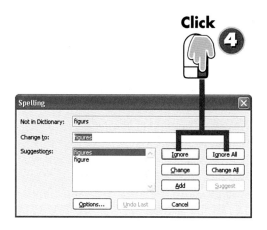

5 **Click**

4 If a word that has been flagged is spelled correctly, click **Ignore Once** or **Ignore All** to skip the word.

5 Continue changing or ignoring all the flagged words. When the spelling check is complete, Outlook notifies you by displaying a message box; click **OK**.

End

Adding a Word to the Dictionary
If Outlook has flagged a word that is not misspelled, and it is a word that you commonly use, you can add it to Outlook's dictionary so that it won't be flagged the next time you use it. To do so, click the **Add to Dictionary** button in the Spelling dialog box.

Automatically Correcting a Word
If you often misspell a particular word and want to have Outlook automatically correct it, select or type the correct spelling in the Spelling dialog box and click AutoCorrect.

Changing the Appearance of Text

Start

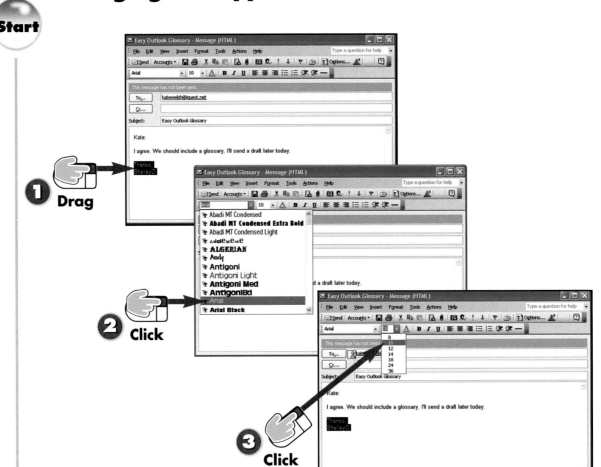

1 Drag

2 Click

3 Click

1. After you've created a new message, completing the To and Subject fields and typing the message text, select the text whose formatting you want to change.

2. Click the **down-arrow** button to the right of the **Font** field on the Message window's toolbar and select a new font from the list that appears.

3. The font you chose is applied to the selection. To change the font size, click the **down-arrow** button to the right of the **Font Size** field on the Message window's toolbar and select a new size from the list that appears.

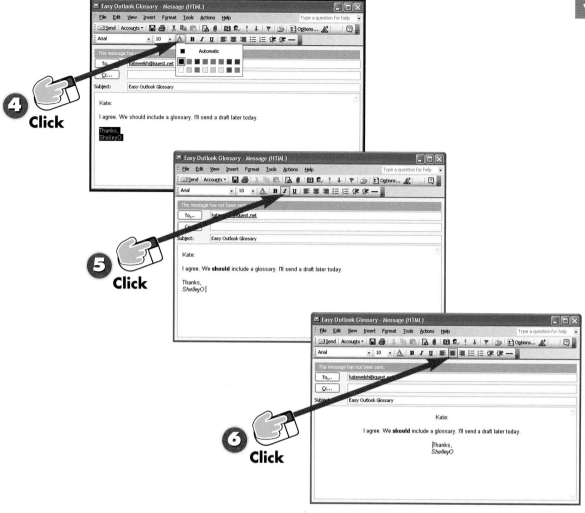

4 The font size you chose is applied to the selection. To change the color of the selected text, click the **down arrow** next to the **Font Color** button on the Message window's toolbar and select a new color from the list that appears.

5 The color you chose is applied to the selection. To make the selected text bold, italic, or underlined, click the appropriate button or buttons.

6 To change the text alignment, click the **Left**, **Center**, or **Right** button. (Here, the entire message is centered; if you have selected text, only that text is aligned.)

7 When you are finished formatting the message, send it as usual.

End

Options Not Available?

If any of these formatting options are not available, it's because they are not supported by the mail format you have selected. For example, if you've configured Outlook to send messages in Plain Text format, you will not be able to apply new fonts, font sizes, colors, or styles to your messages. For information about changing to a different mail format, see the task "Selecting an E-mail Format."

Don't Type in ALL CAPS!

A word on Netiquette: It is considered rude to type in all CAPS, as your recipients may view it as the equivalent of screaming.

Using Word to Create E-mail Messages

Start

Click **1**

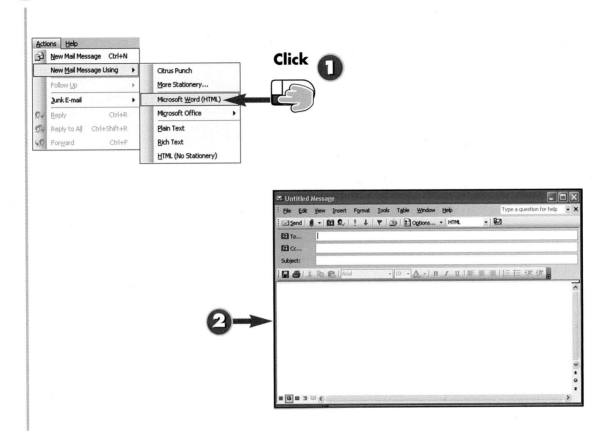

2

1 Open the **Actions** menu, choose **New Mail Using**, and select **Microsoft Word (HTML)**.

2 Outlook opens what looks like a standard Message window, but it is in fact a Microsoft Word window.

Outlook enables you to use Microsoft Word to create e-mail messages; using Word provides many more options for formatting the message than Outlook does. You can choose more fonts, change alignments, use color, and make other common text and paragraph appearance changes.

TIP

Recipient Can't View Your Message?
For the people who receive your message to be able to properly view it, their mail program must support HTML format (most do). If a recipient has problems, however, try sending the message in plain-text format. See "Selecting an E-mail Format."

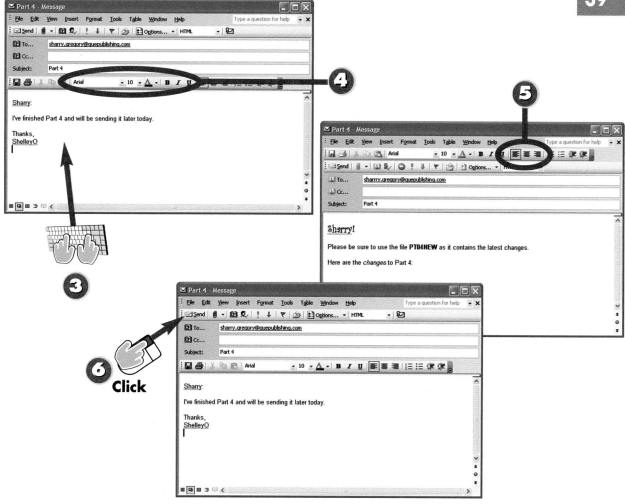

3. Just as you would in a regular e-mail message, complete the address information, type a subject, and type the message.

4. Using the Formatting toolbar or the Format menu, make changes as needed to the appearance of the text, such as changing the font.

5. Make any formatting changes to the paragraph alignment, such as indenting text or adding bullets.

6. Click the **Send** button. The message is sent.

End

Setting Word as the Default

You can select Word as the default program for creating e-mail messages. For more information, see "Setting the Default Mail Format" later in this part.

Selecting an E-mail Format

Start

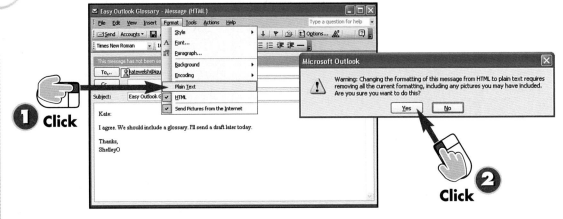

① Click

② Click

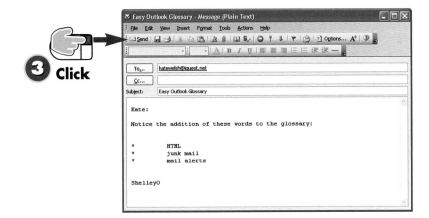

③ Click

① After you've created a new message, open the **Format** menu. The current message format is indicated with a check mark; to change it, choose the format you want to use (in this case, **Plain Text**).

② If you have already typed the text for your message, Outlook notifies you that any formatting applied to your text will be lost; click **Yes** to continue.

③ Text in your message will be stripped of its formatting attributes; send the message as usual.

End

Assigning a Priority to a Message

Start

Click ①

Click ②

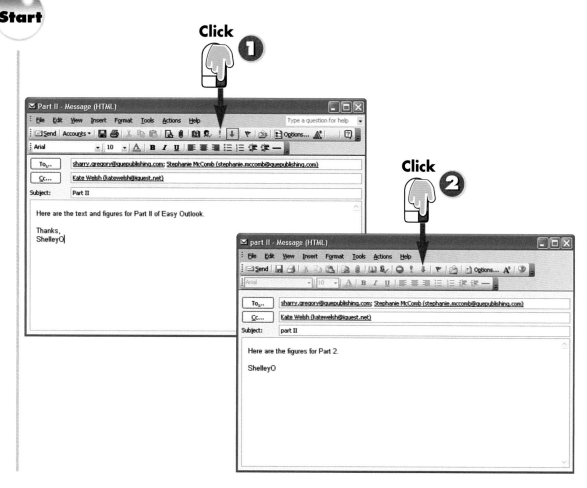

① After you've created a new message, completing the To and Subject fields and typing the message text, click the **Importance: High** button on the Message window's toolbar to mark the message as high priority.

② Click the **Importance: Low** button to mark the message as low priority. (You won't notice anything different about the message itself, but the selected button is high-lighted in the Message window.)

End

INTRODUCTION

Because a person can receive literally hundreds of messages a day, you may want to assign a priority to help the recipient see at a glance the importance of your message. For example, if your message requires immediate attention, you may want to mark a message as important. For messages containing jokes or other low-priority information, on the other hand, you may want to mark the importance as low. When the message is received, the recipient can view its priority in his or her Inbox. (If you assign no priority to an e-mail message, the message will include no importance indicators.)

Caution!

CAUTION

Use the high-importance label sparingly. It's like the old fable about the boy who cried wolf: If you label all your messages as important, your sender may ignore messages that really are important.

Attaching a File to a Message

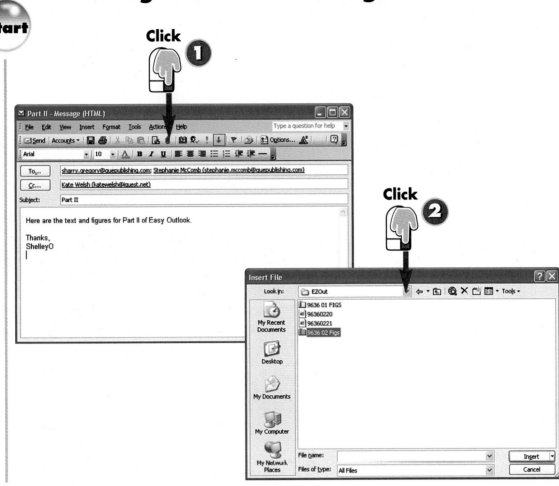

Start

Click ①

Click ②

1. After you've created a new message, completing the To and Subject fields and typing the message text, click the **Insert File** button on the Message window's toolbar.

2. The Insert File dialog box opens, displaying the contents of the My Documents folder. Navigate to the drive and folder that contains the file you want to attach.

INTRODUCTION

In addition to sending text messages, you can attach files to messages. For example, you might send in your expense report to your office, submit a chapter to your editor, or send a picture of your child to his grandparents.

TIP

Finding a File
You can change to another drive or folder by using the Look In drop-down list, the Up One Level button, or the Places bar. You can also double-click any one of the listed folders to open and select files within that folder.

HINT

Downloading Attachments
Depending on the recipient's connection speed, a file attachment can take a while to download. For this reason, you may want to compress the file(s) into a compressed folder before sending.

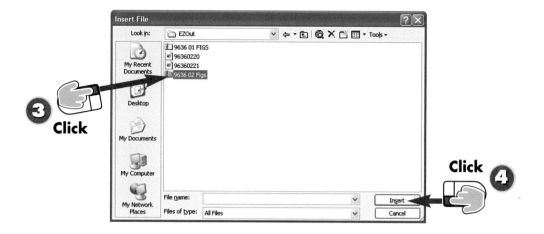

Click

Click **4**

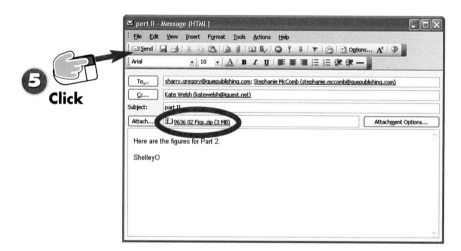

5 **Click**

3 Click the file you want to attach to select it.

4 Click **Insert**.

5 The mail window now includes an Attach box, which lists the file you selected. Send the message as usual by clicking the **Send** button.

End

A Word on File Types
For the recipient to open the file, he or she must have the appropriate software program. For example, if you send a Word document, the recipient must have a program that can open and work with Word documents. If you are not sure, you can save the document using a generic file type such as plain text when you create the actual file.

Removing a File Attachment
To remove a file attachment from an e-mail message, right-click the filename in the message window's Attach box and click **Remove**.

Adding a Web Page Link to a Message

Start

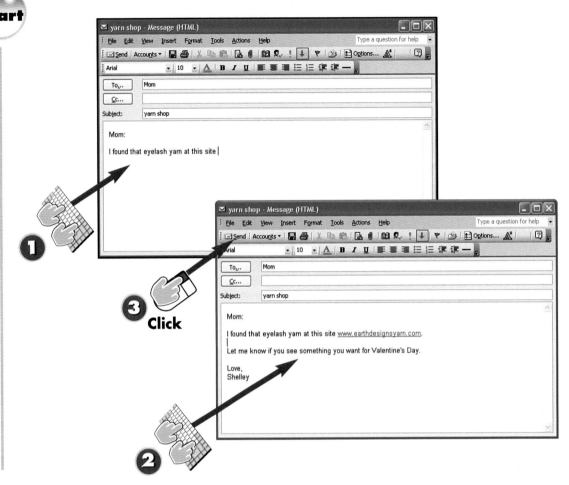

3 **Click**

2

1 Create a new message, completing the To and Subject fields, and begin typing the message text.

2 When you get to the spot in the message text where you want to insert the link, type the Web address of the site (in this example, **www.earthdesignsyarn.com**).

3 Finish typing the message and send it as usual.

End

INTRODUCTION

Your e-mail message is not limited to including only text. In fact, it can include any number of other elements, including links to Web sites. Using Outlook, you can e-mail a link to a site to another person. When that person opens the message, he or she can click the link to go to the site.

TIP

Sending Mail from Internet Explorer
Internet Explorer includes a Mail toolbar button for sending a link or page directly from the Web site. Click this button to create a mail message with the link or page included.

HINT

Pasting the Address
If you prefer, you can copy an address from your Internet browser by first selecting it and then opening the **Edit** menu and choosing the **Copy** command. You can then paste the link into the message using **Edit, Paste**.

Requesting a Receipt

Start

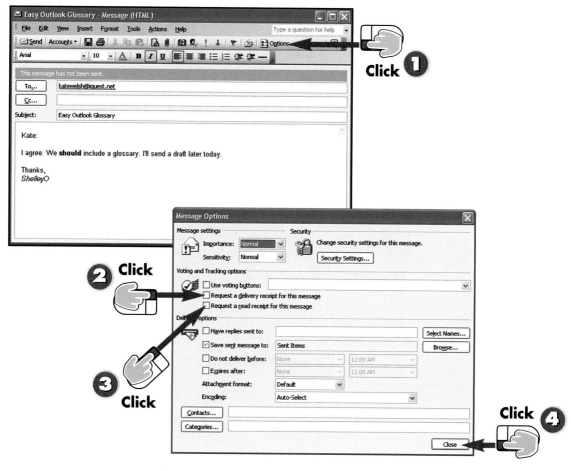

Click ①

② Click

③ Click

Click ④

① After you create a new message, completing the To and Subject fields and typing the message text, click the **Options** button on the Message window's toolbar.

② The Message Options dialog box opens. To request a delivery receipt, click the **Request a Delivery Receipt for This Message** check box to select it.

③ To request a read receipt, click the **Request a Read Receipt for This Message** check box to select it.

④ Click the **Close** (x) button and send the message as usual. When the message is delivered and/or read, you'll receive a confirmation e-mail message.

End

INTRODUCTION

If you want to be sure that someone has received your message, you can request a *delivery receipt.* That way, when the recipient downloads your message from his or her ISP's e-mail server, you receive a message indicating that your e-mail was delivered. In addition, you can request a *read receipt,* which notifies you when your message is opened by the recipient.

CAUTION

No Receipt Received?
If you've requested a receipt but don't receive one, it doesn't necessarily mean your message wasn't delivered or read. Some e-mail programs do not send delivery or read receipts.

Saving a Message to Send Later

Start

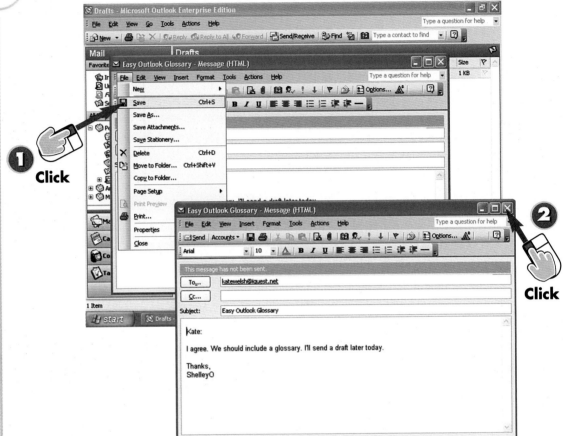

Click

Click

1 After you create a rough draft of a message, open the **File** menu and choose **Save**.

2 Close the message by clicking its **Close** (×) button. The message is saved in the Drafts folder.

TIP

Holding Off on "Hot" Messages

If your emotions are riding high, it's a good idea to wait before you send an e-mail message. It can be easy to misconstrue the tone of an e-mail message without voice, facial expressions, and other elements that are in play for face-to-face or even telephone conversations. So be safe rather than sorry!

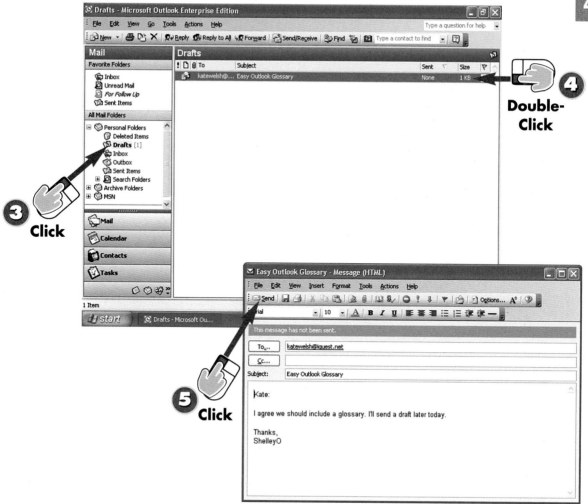

Double-Click

Click

Click

3 To open a saved message, click the **Drafts** folder in the All Mail Folders list. (You can tell that the Draft folder contains unsent messages because its name is bold; the number of messages it contains is indicated in parentheses.)

4 Double-click the message in the Drafts message list.

5 Make changes to the message as needed and then send the message as usual.

End

Forget to Save?
If you close a message without sending or saving it, Outlook prompts you to save it. Click **Yes** to save a copy of the message in the Drafts folder.

Cancel Message
If you want to close and cancel a message, click the Message window's **Close** (×) button. Outlook will ask whether you want to save the message; click **No**.

Checking Sent Messages

Start

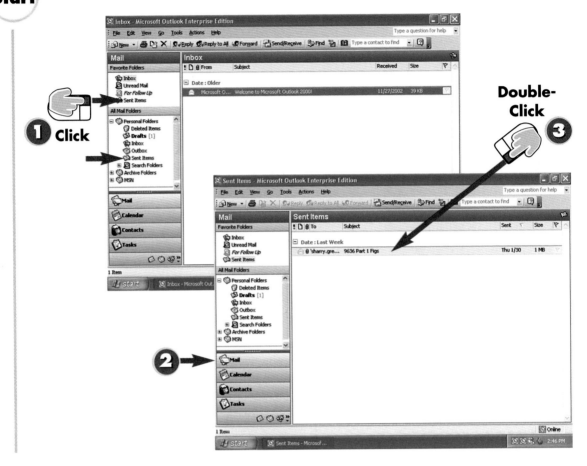

Click

Double-Click

1 Click the **Sent Items** folder under either Favorite Folders or All Mail Folders.

2 A list of all the messages you have sent appears.

3 To open a message, double-click it in the Sent Items mail list.

End

Working Offline

Start

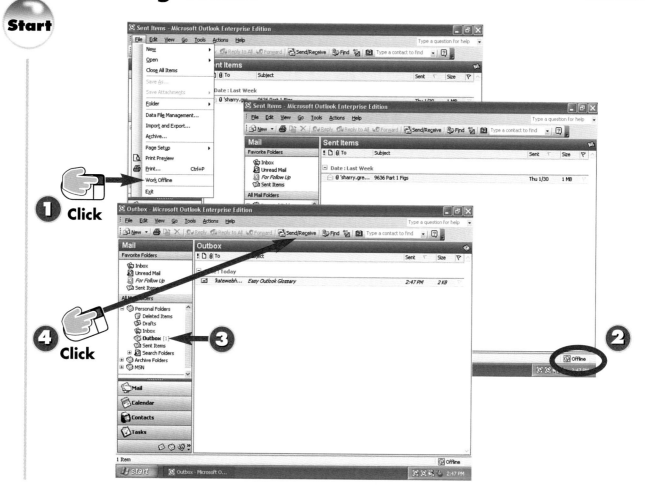

1 Click

4 Click

3

2

1. Open the **File** menu and select **Work Offline**.

2. Note that the status bar displays the Offline icon. Create new messages (and reply to existing ones) as usual. Click **Send** after finishing each message.

3. Messages you send are stored in the Outbox.

4. To go back online and send the messages, click the **Send/Receive** button in the Outlook toolbar.

End

INTRODUCTION

If you have several messages to review and create, you may prefer to work offline. That way, you can create all the messages, go online, and send them all at once. You might use this method if you do not have a separate connection for your Internet access.

TIP

After Messages Are Sent
By default, Outlook goes back offline after sending all the messages in your Outbox.

Reading and Handling E-mail Messages

In addition to creating e-mail, you can use Outlook to manage your incoming mail. Not only can you read your messages, you can choose how to handle them. Some messages you may want to print; others you might choose to delete. In addition, you can save messages and file attachments. This part concentrates on all of Outlook's mail-handling features.

Handling Your Mail in Outlook

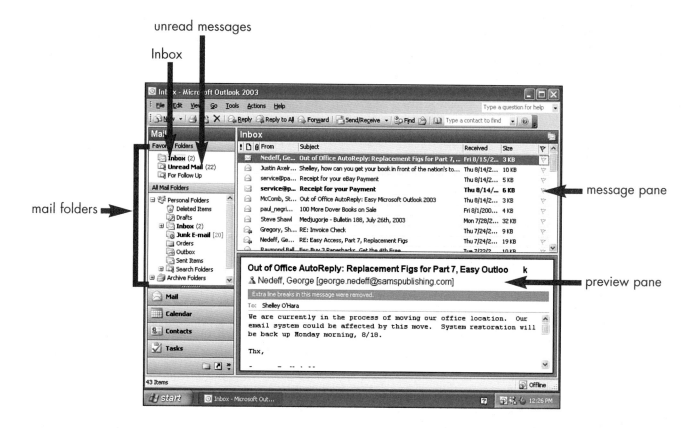

unread messages

Inbox

mail folders →

message pane

preview pane

Receiving and Reading Messages

Start

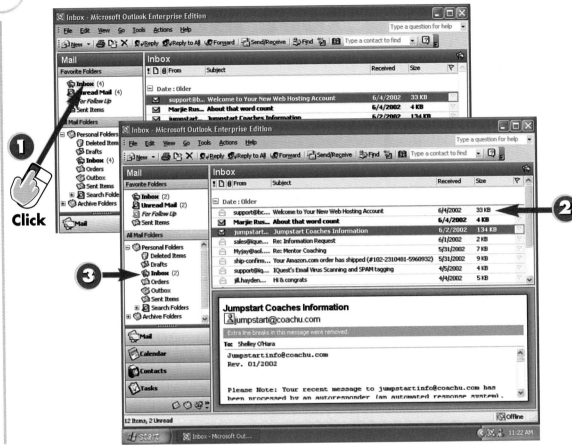

Click

1. With Outlook open on your desktop, click **Inbox** under Favorite Folders or All Mail Folders to go to your Inbox.

2. If you have set up Outlook to automatically log on and receive messages, you see any new messages you've received in the message list in bold.

3. The Inbox is also marked in bold and lists the number of new messages you've received.

If you have an e-mail address, you can both send and receive messages. To read your mail, simply log on to your e-mail provider; the messages sent to you (and stored temporarily on the mail provider's network) are copied to your computer. You can then open and read your messages.

Connecting Manually

If you have set up Outlook for manual connection, click the **Send/Receive** button, log on, and download your e-mail messages. Part 4, "Using Advanced Mail Features," covers how to specify when messages are sent.

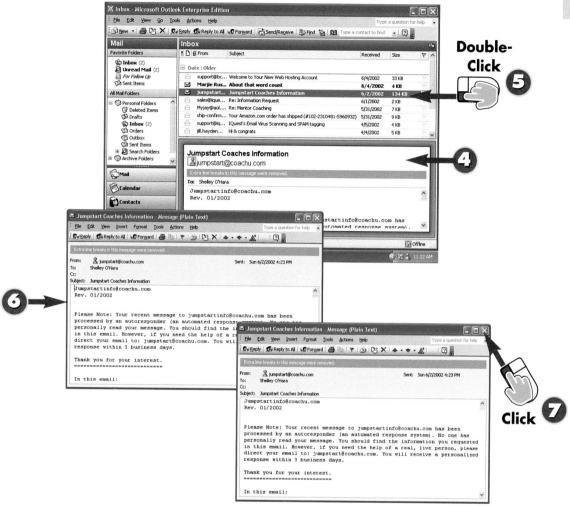

Double-Click 5

4

6

Click 7

④ If the Preview pane is displayed, you see a preview of the selected message.

⑤ To open a message, double-click it in the Inbox list.

⑥ The message is displayed in its own window.

⑦ When you are finished reading the message, click its **Close** (×) button to close the window.

End

Displaying the Preview Pane

If the Preview pane is not displayed in your Outlook window, turn it on by opening the **View** menu and choosing **Preview Pane**. Then, specify where it should be placed by selecting **Right** or **Bottom** from the submenu. (Click **Off** to turn off this pane.)

Ignoring Unsolicited Mail

You'll receive a lot of unsolicited mail. As a rule, do not open a message if you do not recognize the sender because it may contain a virus.

Replying to a Message

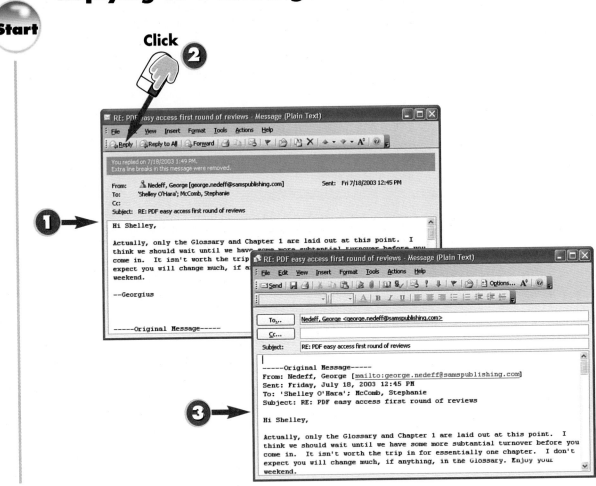

Start

Click 2

1. Open the message you want to reply to.

2. Click the **Reply** button in the mail window's toolbar.

3. Outlook creates a new message, completing the To and Subject lines. (**Re:** is added to the Subject line to indicate that this message is a reply.)

Outlook makes it easy to reply to a message you have received. When you reply, the recipient's address is completed, as well as the Subject line. The text of the original message is included as well. You can continue an ongoing e-mail conversation by replying to messages.

Replying to All Recipients
If the message was sent to several people and you want to reply to all the recipients, click the **Reply to All** button in step 2.

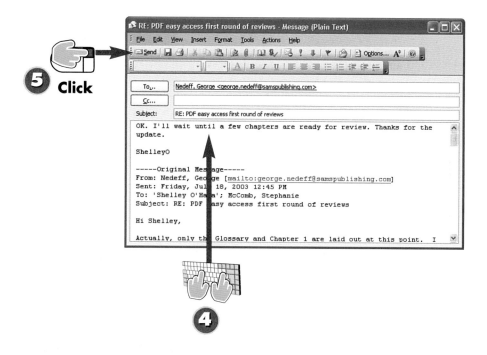

⑤ Click

④ Type your response.

⑤ Click the **Send** button in the message window's toolbar. The message is sent.

End

Forwarding a Message

Start

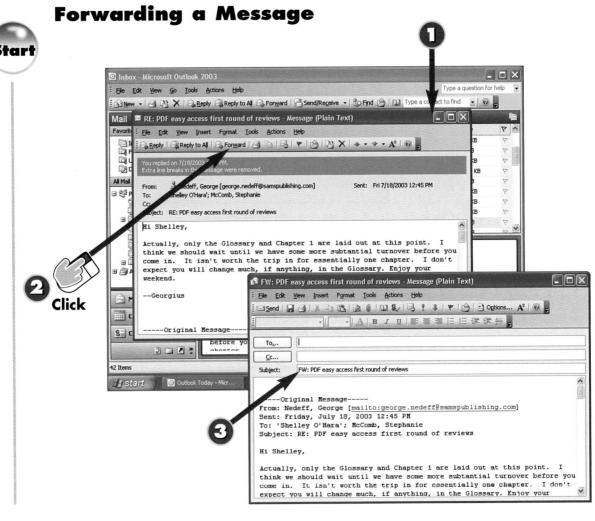

2 Click

1. Open the message you want to forward.

2. Click the **Forward** button.

3. Outlook creates a new message, completing the Subject line. (**Fw:** is added to the Subject line to indicate that the message has been forwarded.)

Suppose you've received a message, such as a funny joke, that you want to send, or forward, to someone else. In that case, you can use Outlook's Forward feature.

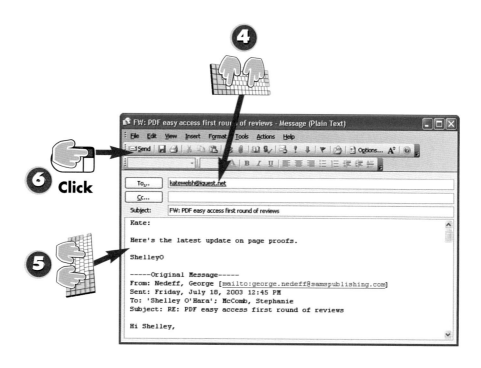

④ Enter the recipient(s) address(es) by typing it in the **To** line or by clicking the **To** button and selecting it from the Address Book.

⑤ Type any additional message you want to include.

⑥ Click the **Send** button in the message window's toolbar. The message is sent.

Forwarding from the Inbox
As an alternative, you can forward a message from the Inbox. You follow the same basic procedure as outlined here, but you select the message in the Inbox and then click the **Forward** button in the Outlook window's toolbar.

Viewing Other Messages

Start

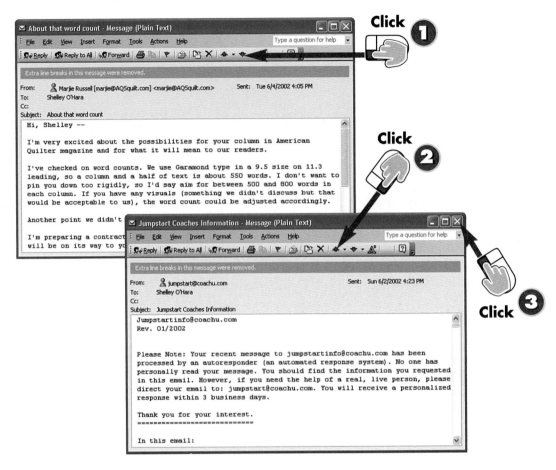

Click ①

Click ②

Click ③

① After you've double-clicked a message in the Inbox to open it, click the **Next Item** button on the message window's toolbar to display the next message.

② The next message in the Inbox list is displayed. Click the **Previous Item** button to display the previous message.

③ The previous message in the Inbox list is displayed. Click the message window's **Close** (×) button to close the message and return to the Inbox.

End

Rather than return to the Inbox to open each message, you can automatically display the next (or previous) message in the Inbox list from within an open message window.

Displaying Other Messages
You can display other messages, including the last message in the Inbox folder, by clicking the **down arrow** next to the **Next Item** or **Previous Item** button and then clicking the desired item.

Sorting Messages

Start

2 Click

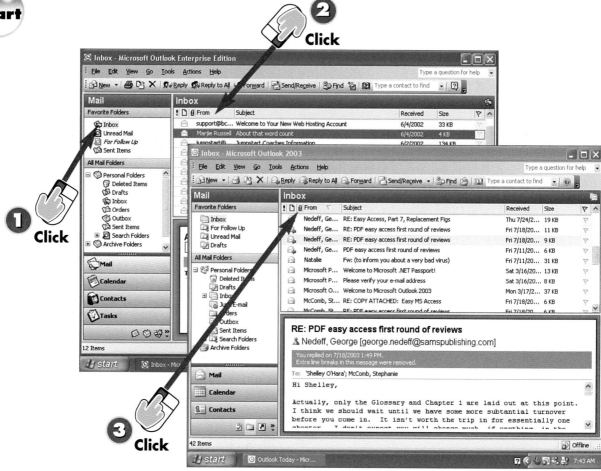

1 Click

3 Click

---

1 Click the folder whose content you want to sort.

2 Click the heading of the column by which you want to sort. For example, to sort by sender, click the **From** column header.

3 Messages are sorted by sender. To change the sort order from ascending to descending or vice versa, click the column heading (in this case, **From**) again.

End

INTRODUCTION

Mail can quickly pile up in your mail folders, making it difficult to find a particular message. By default, Outlook lists messages in date order, but you can change how messages are sorted to suit your needs. For example, you can sort by subject or sender and in ascending or descending order.

TIP

Expanding and Collapsing Messages
To collapse a group of messages, displaying only the category or group name, click the minus sign (–) next to the message group. To expand the group to show all messages in that group, click the plus sign (+).

Printing a Message

Start

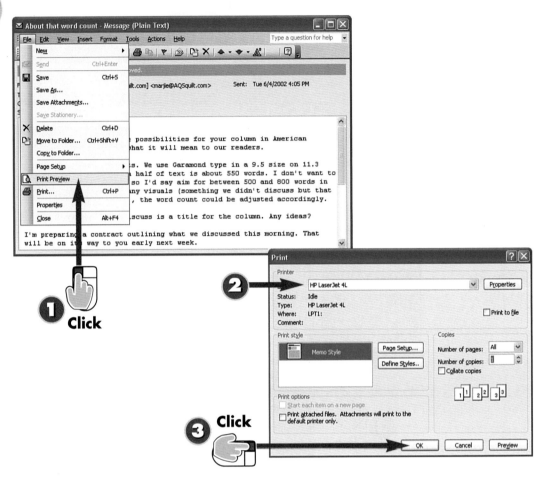

1 Click

2

3 Click

End

1 After you've opened the message you want to print, open the **File** menu and choose **Print**.

2 Select a printer, a print style, the number of copies you want to print, and any other print options.

3 Click **OK**. The message is printed.

INTRODUCTION

Suppose someone e-mails you directions to a party. Fortunately, you can use Outlook to print the message containing the directions; that way, you can take them with you.

TIP

Printing Quickly
If you don't need to change any of the print options, you can bypass the Print dialog box by clicking the **Print** button on the message window's toolbar or by pressing Ctrl+P, the Print shortcut key. You can also print from the Inbox by clicking the message you want to print and then clicking the **Print** button in the Outlook window's main toolbar.

Deleting a Message

Start

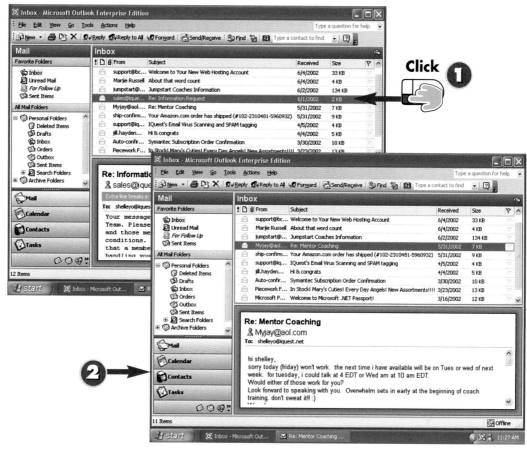

Click ①

②

① In the Inbox (or any other folder), click the message you want to delete. (Alternatively, open the message.)

② The message is removed from the Inbox and placed in the Deleted Items folder.

End

To keep your mail folders, especially your Inbox, organized, you should delete any messages you do not need. When you delete a message, it is moved from the Inbox to the Deleted Items folder. You can undelete a message if needed (see the next task).

Permanently Deleting Messages
To permanently delete a message, open the **Deleted Items** folder and click the message to select it. Click the **Delete** button in the Outlook window's main toolbar; when prompted to confirm the permanent deletion, click **Yes**.

Undeleting a Message

Start

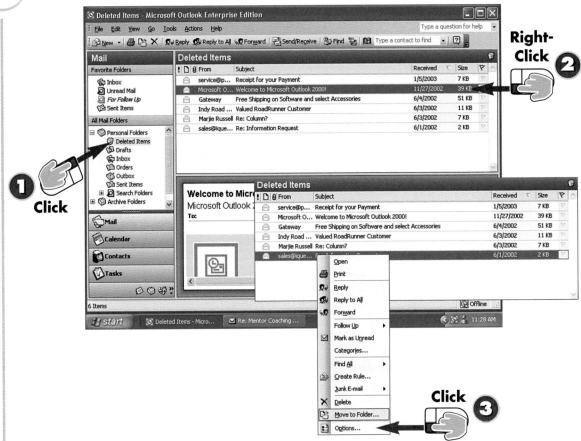

Right-Click ②

Click ①

Click ③

① Click the **Deleted Items** folder in the All Mail Folders list.

② You see the contents of the Deleted Items folder. Right-click the item you want to undelete.

③ Click **Move to Folder** in the shortcut menu that appears.

If you delete a message by mistake, you can retrieve it. As mentioned, Outlook does not delete a message, but simply moves it to the Deleted Items folder. You can open this folder and move the deleted message back to your Inbox or other folder. (This task works not only for messages but for any Outlook item you delete, such as a contact record, an appointment, and so on.)

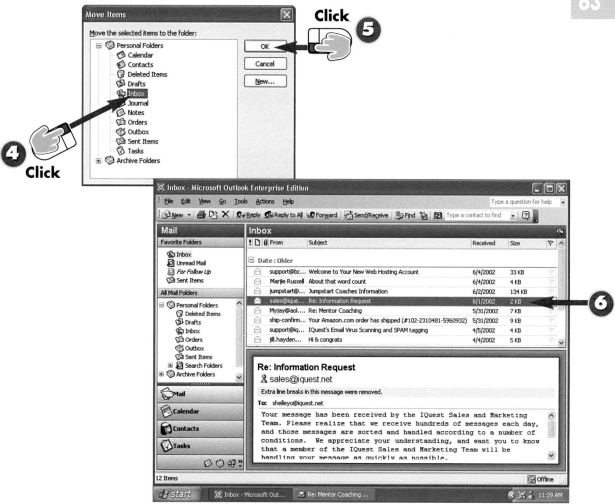

Click 5

Click 4

4 The Move Items dialog box opens. Click the folder to which you want to move the deleted item.

5 Click **OK**.

6 The item is removed from the Deleted Items folder and is moved to the folder you selected—in this case, the Inbox. (You can open the Inbox to confirm that the move occurred.)

End

Emptying the Deleted Items Folder
You should periodically empty the Deleted Items folder to regain the space used to store these items. First, check that the folder doesn't contain any items you need. Then open the **Tools** menu and choose **Empty Deleted Items Folder**.

Moving Messages
When you undelete a message, you can move it back to its original folder, or to another folder altogether. For example, you might set up your own folders to keep mail organized and move deleted items to any of these folders.

Opening File Attachments

Start

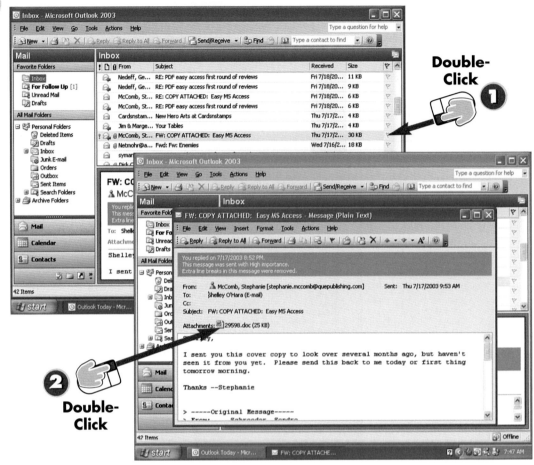

Double-Click 1

Double-Click 2

① Display the message that contains the file attachment. (Messages with attachments are indicated with a paper clip icon.) Then Double-click the message to open it.

② Double-click the attachment to open it.

Sometimes you will receive file attachments as part of a message. For example, your daughter might send you a digital photograph of your grandchild. You can then open and save this file.

Avoiding Viruses

File attachments sent with e-mail messages can contain viruses, which can cause problems on your computer. It's a good idea to use a virus-checking program such as Norton's Anti-Virus to scan any attachments for viruses . Also, never open attachments from senders you don't recognize.

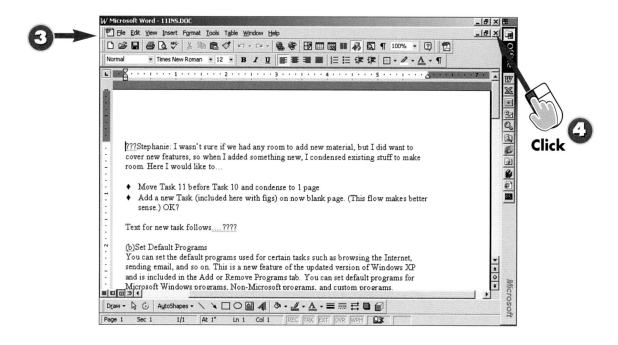

Click

3 Outlook starts the associated program and opens and displays the file.

4 The file is stored in a temporary folder when it is opened. (To save the file, see the next task.) When you are finished viewing the file, click the **Close** (x) button.

End

Specifying the Correct Program
If Outlook doesn't know which program to use to open the file, you are prompted to select the program.

Handling Forwarded Messages
Often, messages that have been forwarded are sent as attachments. You may have to double-click the message attachment several times to open the actual message.

Saving File Attachments

Start

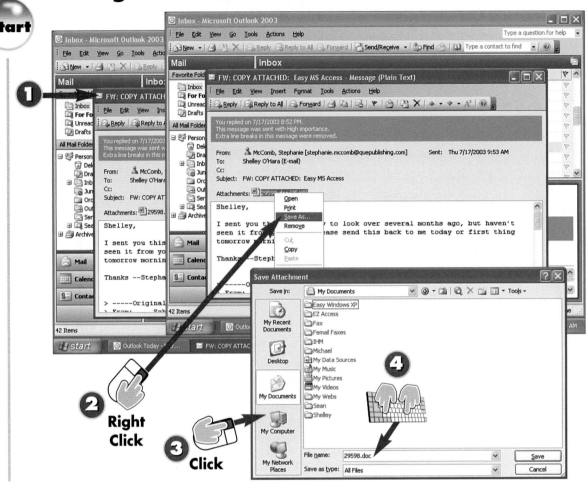

2 Right Click

3 Click

4

---

1 Open the message that contains the file attachment you want to save.

2 Right-click the file attachment and click **Save As** in the menu that appears.

3 In the Save Attachment dialog box, select the drive and folder in which you want to save the file.

4 If desired, type a new filename.

If you are sent an attachment, you may want to save it. You can specify the drive and folder in which the file will be saved, as well as change the filename if needed. You can still open the file, only now it is named and saved on your hard drive rather than in a temporary folder.

Changing Drives and Folders
Use the **Save In** drop-down list, the **Places** bar, or the **Up One Level** button to change to another drive or folder. You can also double-click any listed folder to open and save the attachment to that folder.

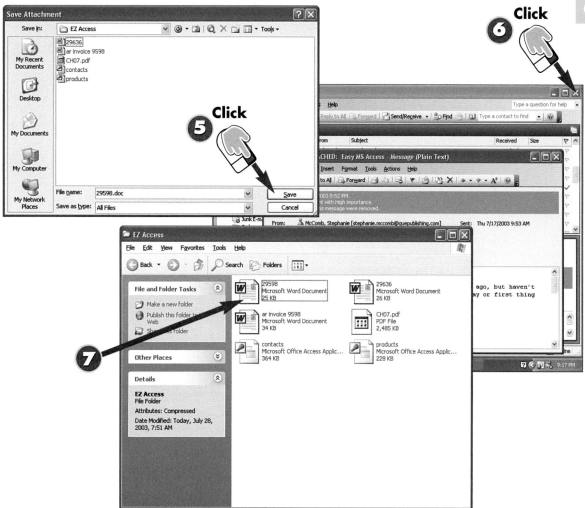

5 Click the **Save** button. The file is saved.

6 Click the message window's **Close** (x) button to close the message.

7 Open the drive and folder that contains the saved file attachment to confirm you saved it.

End

Checking for Viruses

Just because you save a file to your computer, it does not mean that it can't contain a virus. You should still use a virus-scanning program such as Norton's Anti-Virus to check the file attachment for any viruses.

Associating Programs

For you to be able to view or edit a saved file, your computer must have installed on it a program capable of handling that file. For example, if the file is a Microsoft Word document, you'll need to have Word (or another word-processing program capable of opening Word files) installed on your own computer to view or edit the file. If no program on your computer is associated with the file you've saved, Outlook will prompt you to select the program you want to use to open the file.

Finding a Message

Start

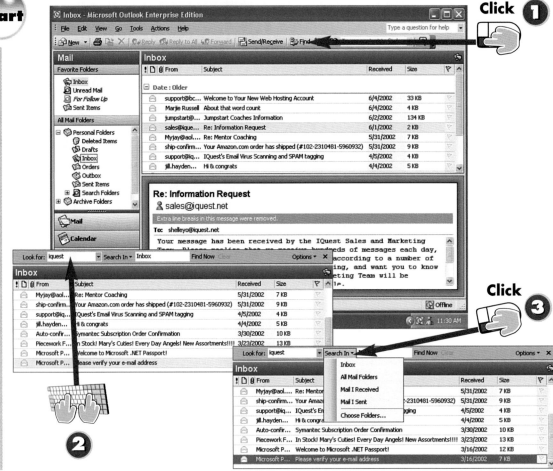

Click **1**

Click **3**

2

1 To begin searching, click the **Find** button in the main Outlook toolbar. The Find bar is displayed under the toolbar.

2 Type the text you want to search by, such as the name of the sender or the text in the subject line.

3 Outlook searches in the current folder by default. To select another folder, click the **down arrow** next to the **Search In** drop-down list and specify where to search.

If you cannot find a message by scrolling or sorting, you can search for it. You can search on any number of criteria including the subject, the sender name, the receipt date, and more. If you have many messages or if you received a message a long time ago, search to find it.

Click 4

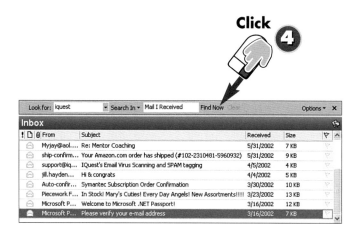

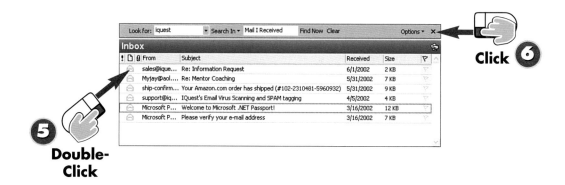

Click 6

5 **Double-Click**

4 Click the **Find Now** button in the Find bar.

5 Outlook searches the selected folders and displays any items that match your criteria. If the search has yielded a match, double-click the message to open it.

6 Click the Find bar's **Close** (×) button to close the Search Results window.

End

Searching All Folders
If you want to search a folder—including any subfolders it contains—or if you want to search multiple folders, click **Choose Folders** from the Search In drop-down list on the Find bar. The Select Folder(s) dialog box opens; select any folders you want to search. To search a folder and all folders within that folder, select the **Search Subfolders** check box. Click **OK**.

Saving a Search
If you often perform the same search, you can save it in Outlook's Search folders. To do so, click the **Options** button in the Find bar and select **Save Search as Search Folder**. Part 4 covers using search folders in more detail.

PART 3

Selecting Messages

Start

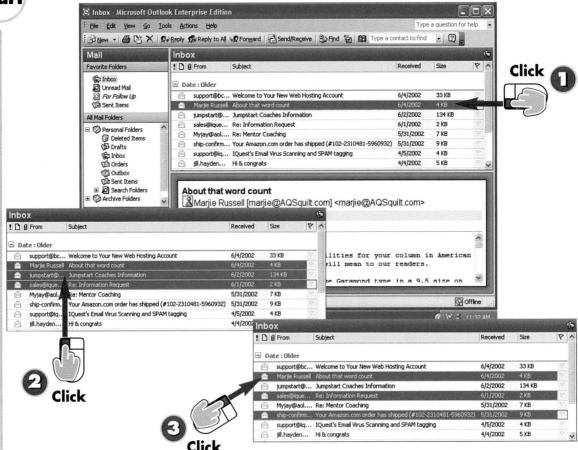

Click 1

2 Click

3 Click

1 To select one message, click it.

2 To select messages listed next to each other, click the first message, press and hold down the **Shift** key, and click the last message. The first, last, and all messages in between are selected.

3 To select messages that are not next to each other, click the first message. Press and hold down the **Ctrl** key, and then click each additional message you want to select.

End

INTRODUCTION

When you want to print, delete, mark, or make other changes to a message, you must first select it. You can select a single message or a group of messages. When selecting a group of messages, they can be listed next to each other or be listed noncontiguously.

Selection Tips
To deselect a message, click outside the selected message. To select all messages in a folder, first display the folder, and then open the **Edit** menu and click **Select All**.

Marking Messages

Start

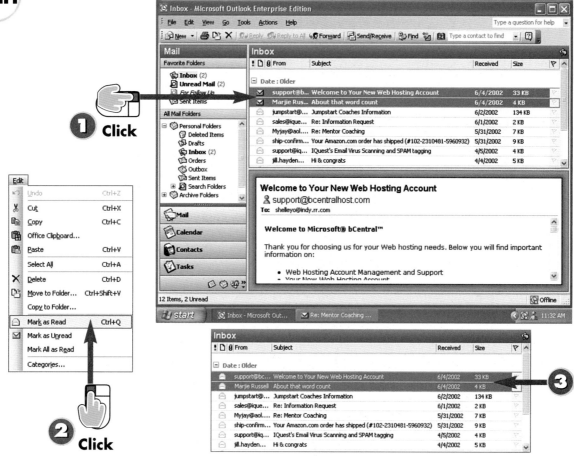

1 Click

2 Click

1 Select the message(s) you want to mark.

2 Open the **Edit** menu and choose **Mark as Read**.

3 The messages are marked as read.

End

INTRODUCTION

Messages that have not been read are displayed in bold, but you can easily enable or disable this marking. For example, you might delete unread junk mail. So that the Deleted Items folder and the messages in it aren't displayed in bold, you can mark them as read.

Marking Messages as Unread
You can also do the reverse—mark a message as unread. You might do this if you opened a message but didn't thoroughly read the contents. To mark a message as unread, select the message, open the **Edit** menu, and choose **Mark as Unread**.

Flagging Messages for Action

Start

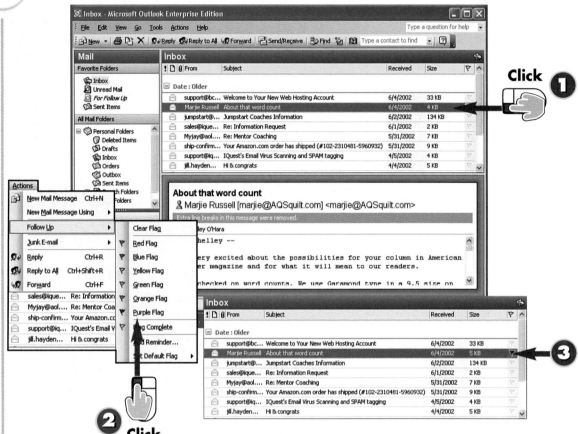

Click ①

Click ②

③

① Select the message you want to flag.

② Open the **Actions** menu and choose **Follow Up**. A submenu containing a list of available follow-up flags appears; click the flag you want to assign.

③ The message is flagged with the color you chose.

You should get in the habit of handling messages as you receive them, removing them from your Inbox. If a message can't be handled immediately, however, you can flag it for action. You can then easily find messages that require your attention. Flagged messages are placed in the For Follow Up folder.

Clearing a Flag
One way to remove a flag is to select the flagged message and then choose **Actions, Follow Up, Clear Flag**. Alternatively, you can mark the follow-up activity as complete, using a completed flag. To do so, select the message, and then choose **Actions, Follow Up, Flag Complete**.

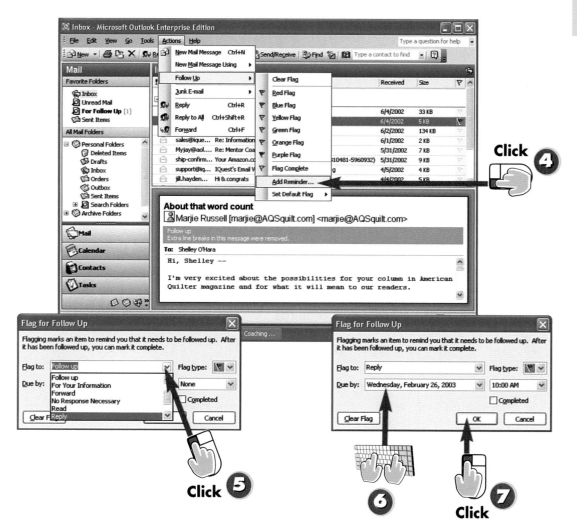

Click 4

Click 5

6

7 **Click**

4 To set a reminder for the flag (that is, to note what action you need to perform for follow up), open the **Actions** menu, choose **Follow Up**, and click **Add Reminder**.

5 The Flag for Follow Up dialog box opens. Click the **down arrow** next to the **Flag To** field and select the appropriate follow-up action from the list that appears.

6 If needed, enter the deadline date and time.

7 Click **OK**. The flag is set, as is the reminder you entered.

End

Organizing Mail
In addition to flagging, Outlook provides several other ways to keep your messages organized. For example, you can move messages to folders, use colors, or assign categories. Part 4 covers these options.

Viewing Flagged Messages
To easily find all flagged messages, open the **For Follow Up** folder. Alternatively, sort on the Flag column. To do so, click the **Flag** column in the mail folder. If you assigned different-colored flags to different messages, each flag type is listed together. You can then easily work with any flagged message.

Using Advanced Mail Features

Because e-mail is probably the most often-used feature of Outlook, it should come as no surprise that there's a wealth of e-mail features worth learning about. Spend some time organizing your messages so that you can easily find and handle messages that require your attention. Consider putting some options into effect for handling junk mail. For new messages, you might set up a signature. Or you might use stationery for a unique look. This section discusses these and other e-mail features.

Setting Outlook Options and Preferences

Mail Setup Options

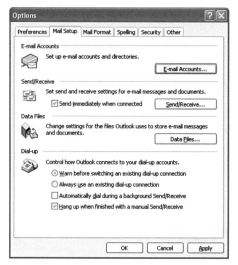

Mail Format Options

Mail Preferences

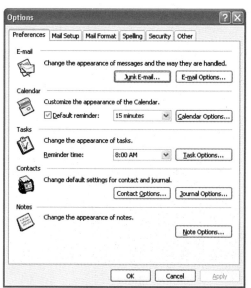

Creating New Folders

Start

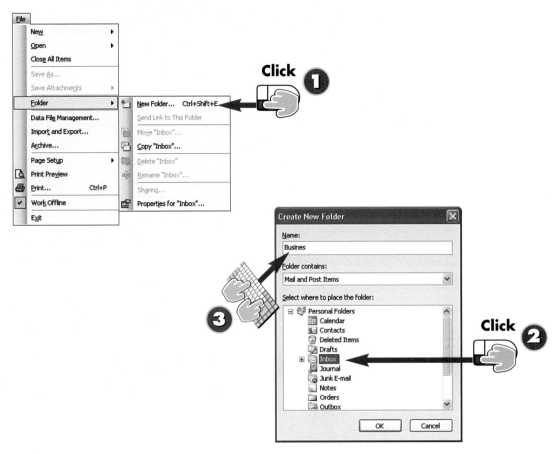

Click ①

Click ②

③

① To create a new folder, open the **File** menu, choose **Folder**, and select **New Folder**.

② The Create New Folder dialog box opens. Click the folder in which you want to place the new folder.

③ Type a name for the new folder in the **Name** field.

In addition to using Outlook's default folders, you can create your own folders. For example, you might create folders for messages that you want to save—one for business correspondence and one for personal mail. Alternatively, if you frequently correspond with several people, you might create a folder for each person and store messages to and from each person in his or her own folder.

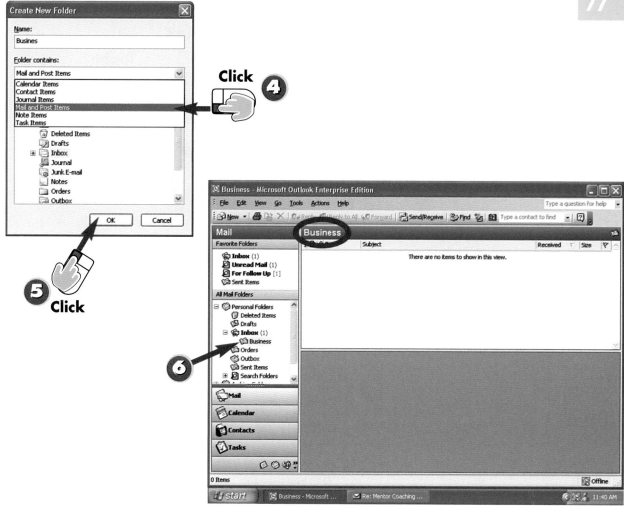

4 To specify what you intend to store in this folder, click the **down arrow** next to the **Folder Contains** field and choose an entry from the list that appears.

5 Click **OK**.

6 The folder is added.

Folder Placement

To place the folder at the same organizational level as the default mail folders, select **Personal Folders** in step 2. To nest the folder within an existing mail (or other) folder, select that folder. For example, to create a subfolder within your Inbox, select **Inbox** in step 2.

Moving Messages

After you have set up a new folder, you can move existing messages into that folder to keep your messages organized. See the task "Organizing Messages in Folders" for help moving messages.

Adding and Removing Folders from the Favorite Folders List

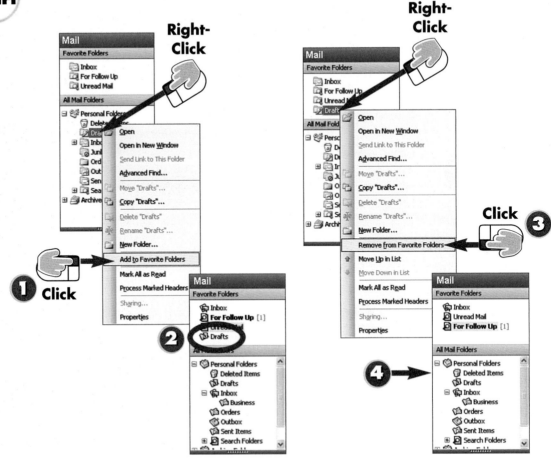

1. In the All Mail Folders list, right-click the folder you want to add to your Favorite Folders list and choose **Add to Favorite Folders List** from the menu that appears.

2. The folder is added to the Favorite Folders list.

3. To remove a folder from the Favorite Folders list, right-click the folder you want to remove and choose **Remove from Favorite Folders List** from the menu that appears.

4. The folder is hidden from this list.

If the default folders provided by Outlook are inadequate for your needs, you can easily add folders found in the All Mail Folders list to your Favorite Folders list. Alternatively, if the Favorite Folders list contains a folder you don't use, you can remove it from the list.

Redisplaying Removed Folders

To redisplay any folders you've removed, right-click the folder in the All Mail Folders list and choose **Show in Favorite Folders List** from the menu that appears.

Rearranging Folders in the Favorite Folders List

Start

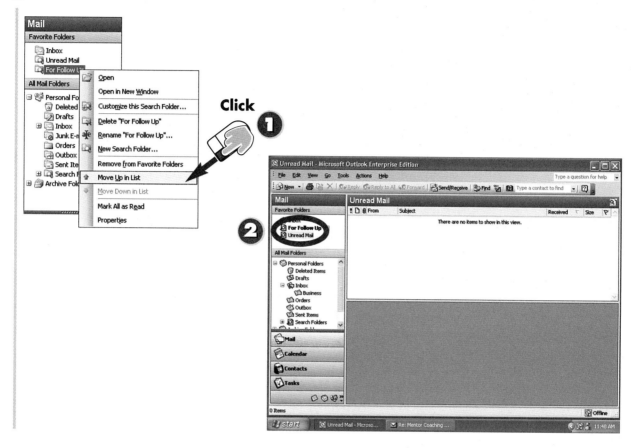

Click

1. Right-click the folder that you want to move and choose **Move Down in List** to move the folder down or **Move Up in List** to move the folder up.

2. The folder is moved.

End

INTRODUCTION

You can change the order of the folders in the Favorite Folders list, putting the folder you use most often at the top of the list. You rearrange the list by selecting an item and then moving it up or down, as needed, to get the order you want.

TIP

Command Not Available?
If the folder you want to move is already at the top of the list, the Move Up in List command will not be available. Likewise, if the folder you want to move is at the bottom of the list, the Move Down in List command will not be available.

Adding a Search Folder

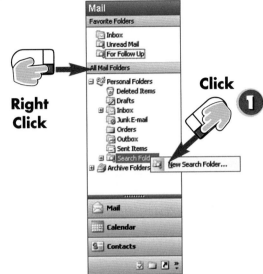

1 Right-click the **Search Folders** folder in the list and then select **New Search Folder** from the shortcut menu that appears.

2 The New Search Folder dialog box opens, displaying a list of several predesigned search folders. If needed, click the scroll buttons to scroll through the list.

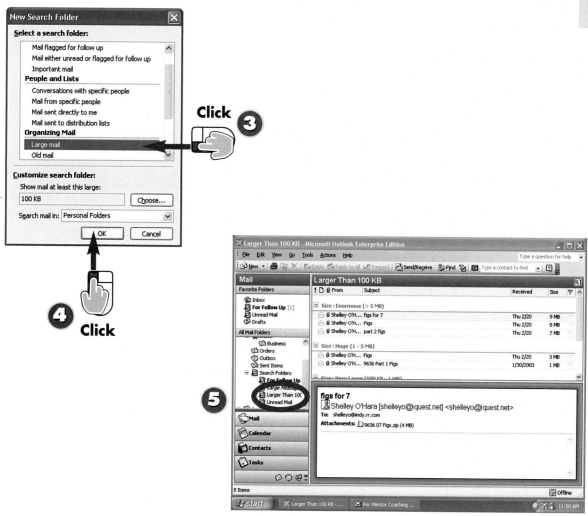

3. Click one of the predesigned search folders to select it.

4. Click **OK**.

5. The new search folder is added to the Search Folders list under All Mail Folders. Outlook also checks any existing messages and includes them in this search folder, along with any new folders that meet the criteria.

End

Customizing Search Folders

When you select a search folder, the **Customize Search Folder** options in the New Search Folder dialog box become available. Click the **Choose** button to view (and, if needed, modify) the criteria for this search folder.

Organizing Messages in Folders

Start

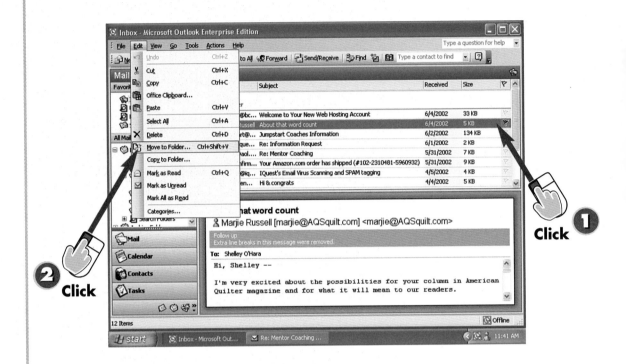

Click ①

② **Click**

---

① Select the message you want to move.

② Open the **Edit** menu and choose **Move to Folder**.

INTRODUCTION

Rather than keeping all your messages in your Inbox, you can delete messages you don't need and move messages you want to keep to folders you have created.

Selecting Messages
For help selecting the messages you want to move, refer to the task "Selecting Messages" in Part 3.

Moving Other Messages
You aren't limited to moving messages only from your Inbox. You can select messages in any folders and move them to other folders.

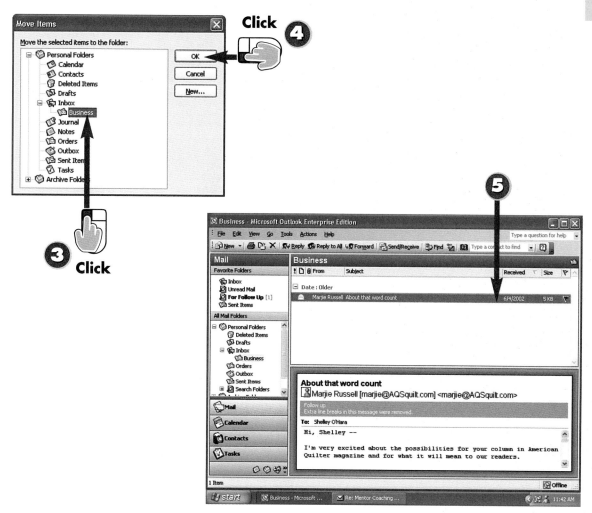

Click 4

3 **Click**

5

3️⃣ The Move Items dialog box opens. Click the folder to which you want to move the selected messages (in this example, the Business folder.)

4️⃣ Click **OK**.

5️⃣ The messages are moved. (To confirm the move, open the folder.)

End

Copying Messages
To copy, rather than move, your message from one folder to another, follow the process outlined in this task, but select **Copy to Folder** instead of **Move to Folder** in step 2.

Using the Toolbar
Instead of opening the Edit menu and choosing Move to Folder, you can click the **Move to Folder** button (the one with two folders on it) on the main Outlook toolbar to open the Move Items dialog box.

Color Coding Messages

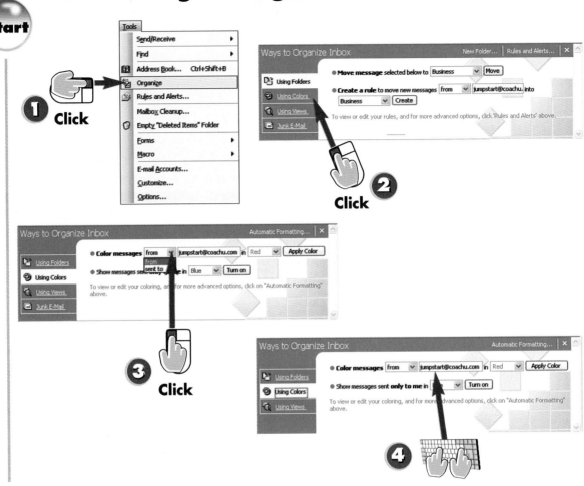

Start

1 Click

2 Click

3 Click

4

1 Open the **Tools** menu and choose **Organize Messages**.

2 The Organize pane opens. Click the **Using Colors** link.

3 Click the **down arrow** next to the **Color Messages** field and choose **From** (to color all messages *from* a particular person) or **Sent To** (to color all messages *to* a particular person).

4 Type the e-mail address of the person whose messages you want to color.

In addition to using folders to organize messages, you can also use colors. For example, you might apply a special color to all messages from a particular person. You can then see at a glance which messages are from that person.

Moving Messages

You can also use the Organize pane to move messages to a different folder. To do so, open the **Tools** menu and choose **Organize**, click the **Using Folders** link, and select the messages you want to move. Display the **Folder** drop-down list, select the folder to which the selected messages should be moved, and click the **Move** button.

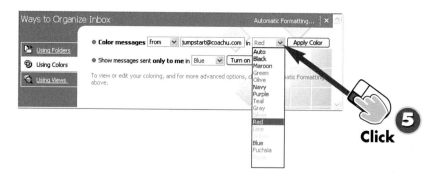

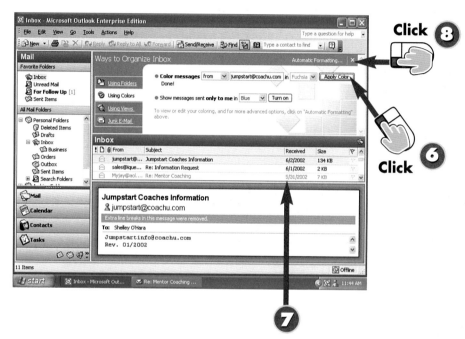

5 Click the **down arrow** next to the **In** field and select the color you want to apply.

6 Click the **Apply Color** button.

7 Messages that match the criteria are displayed in the color you selected.

8 Click the Organize pane's **Close** (x) button to close it.

End

Color Coding Messages Sent to You
If you want to color code messages sent only to you (in contrast to messages that were sent to several individuals), click the **down arrow** next to the **Show Messages Sent Only to Me In** field, choose a color from the list that appears, and then click the **Turn On** button.

Categorizing Messages

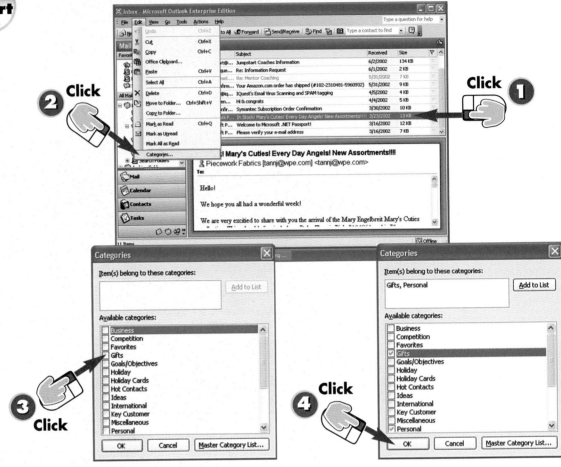

1. Select the message (or messages) to which you want to assign a category.

2. Open the **Edit** menu and choose **Categories**.

3. The Categories dialog box opens. Click the check box next to any categories that should be assigned to the selected message. (You can choose more than one.)

4. The **Item(s) Belong to These Categories** field in the Categories dialog box lists the categories you selected. Click **OK** to assign the categories to the selected messc

End

Emptying the Deleted Items Folder

Start

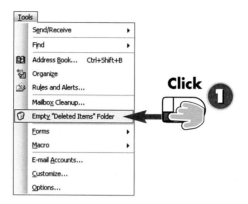

Click ❶

Click ❷

❶ Open the Tools menu and choose **Empty "Deleted Items" Folder**.

❷ Outlook asks whether you're sure you want to empty the folder; click **Yes** to confirm the deletion. The folder is emptied.

End

An important part of keeping your messages organized is deleting those you no longer need. When you learned how to delete messages in Part 3, you also learned that messages you delete are in fact moved to the Deleted Items folder but are not deleted from your system. You should empty this folder periodically to reclaim disk space used by these messages.

INTRODUCTION

Archiving Messages

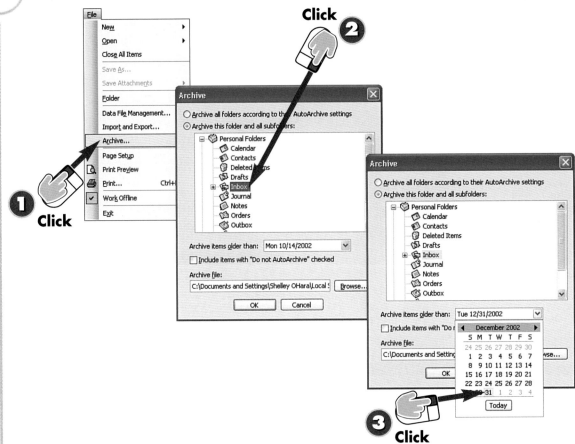

Click

Click

Click

1. Open the **File** menu and choose **Archive**.

2. Select the folder or folders containing messages you want to archive.

3. Click the **down arrow** to the right of the **Archive Items Older Than** field and select a date. Messages in the folder that are older than the selected date will be archived.

If you want to keep older messages, but not have them displayed in your mail folders, you can archive them. Most commonly, you archive messages within a certain date range. If needed, you can display the archived messages at any time.

Viewing Archived Messages

To open and view an archived message, click the plus sign (+) next to Archive Folders in the All Mail Folders list, and then double-click the folder with messages you want to view (deleted items, sent items, and so on) . Those messages are displayed. You can double-click a message to open it.

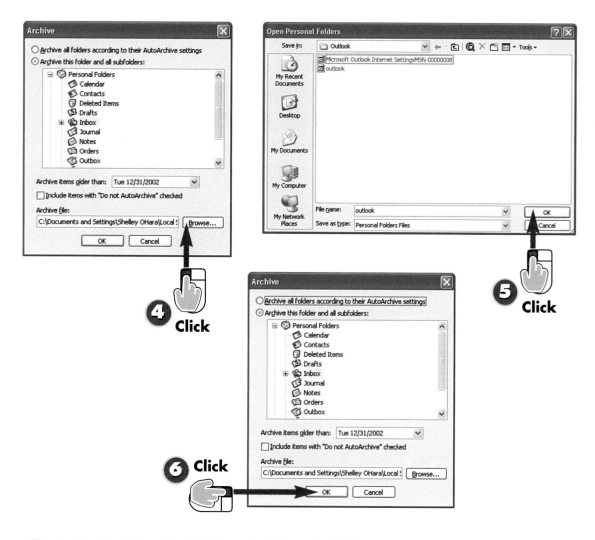

4. In the **Archive File** field, Outlook lists the folder in which the archived messages will be stored by default. To choose a different folder, click the **Browse** button.

5. The Open Personal Folders dialog box opens. Navigate to and select the folder in which you want to archive your messages and click **OK**.

6. Click **OK** in the Archive dialog box. The messages are removed from the mail folders and archived.

End

Viewing AutoArchive Settings

You can use Outlook's AutoArchive settings to automatically archive messages on a set schedule. To do so, open the **Tools** menu, choose **Mailbox Cleanup**, and click the **AutoArchive** button.

More on Mailbox Cleanup

For easy access to tools that will help you keep your mailbox tidy, use Outlook's Mailbox Cleanup dialog box (open the **Tools** menu and choose **Mailbox Cleanup**) . From this dialog box, you can archive messages, empty your Deleted Items folder, and more.

Creating an AutoReply

Start

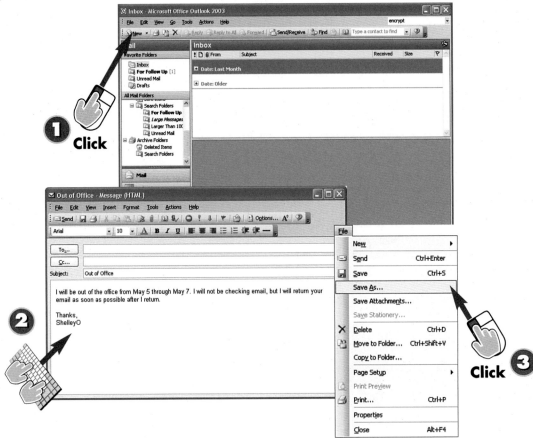

1 Click

2

3 Click

---

1 In the Inbox, click the **New** button on the toolbar in the main Outlook window to create a new mail message.

2 A blank message window opens. Leaving the To field blank, type the autoreply's subject into the Subject field and type the text you want to appear in the message body.

3 Open the **File** menu in the message window and choose **Save As**.

INTRODUCTION

Suppose you will be out of the office and want to alert anyone who sends you an e-mail of that fact so they'll know when they can expect you to respond. In that case, you can set up Outlook to send an autoreply to anyone who sends you a message. This feature is also useful if you change your e-mail address; if someone sends a message to your old address, an autoreply with your new address can be sent. To create an autoreply, you first must create the message that will be sent, saving it as a template.

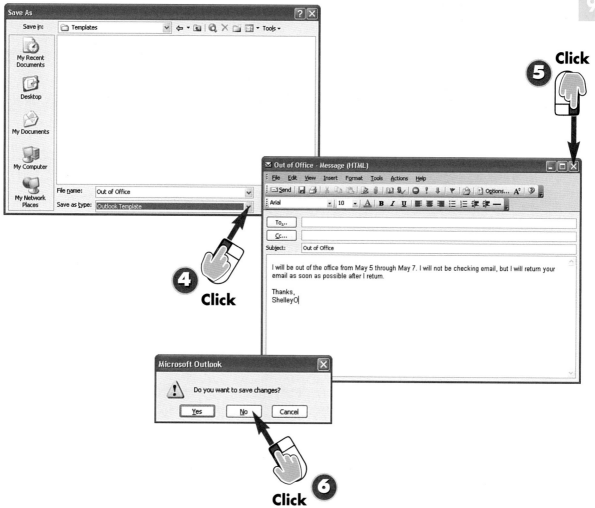

Click

4 Click

Click

6 Click

4 Click the **down arrow** next to the Save As Type field and choose **Outlook Template**. Type a filename for your message in the **File Name** field and click **Save**.

5 Click the **Close** (x) button on the message window to close the message.

6 When prompted to save the message, click **No**.

See
next
page

Saving in the Templates Folder
When you select **Outlook Template** as the file type, Outlook opens the Outlook Template folder in the Save As dialog box, where all Outlook templates are stored.

Creating an AutoReply (continued)

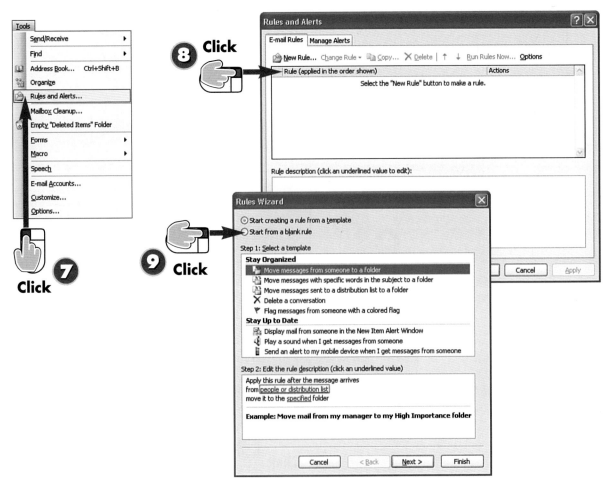

Open the **Tools** menu and choose **Rules and Alerts**.

The Rules and Alerts dialog box opens; click the **New Rule** button.

Outlook launches the Rules Wizard. You can create rules using a template or by starting with a blank rule; for an autoreply, click the **Start from a Blank Rule** option button.

Rules for Sent Messages
You can also create rules for when messages are sent. To see the available options for this type of rule, select **Check Messages After Sending** in the screen shown for step 10, and then follow the wizard steps for this type of rule.

Selecting Other Conditions or Actions
You can build a wide variety of message rules by selecting the appropriate conditions and actions. For instance, for actions, you can select to forward a message, move it, mark it as important, and so on.

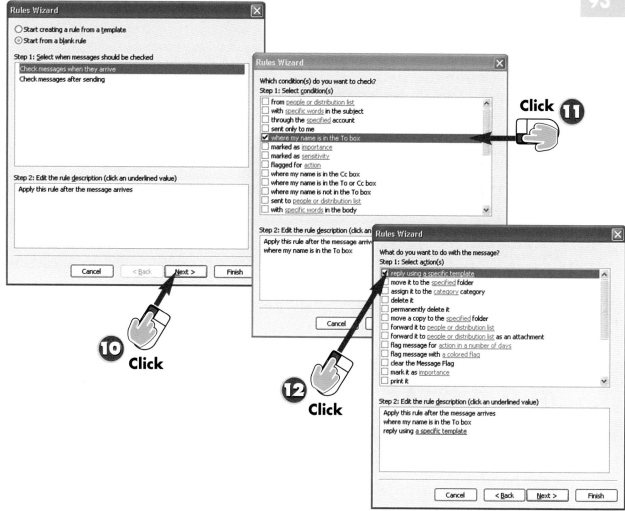

10 The wizard displays the options for creating a blank rule. For step 1, the default is to check messages when they arrive; leave that option selected and click **Next**.

11 Select the conditions for the rule by checking the appropriate check boxes. (Here, the **Where My Name Is in the To Box** check box is checked.) Then click **Next**.

12 Select the action to take when the conditions are met by checking the appropriate check box. (For an autoreply, check **Reply Using a Specific Template**.)

See next page

Creating Other Mail Rules

As you can see, Outlook provides wizards for creating other common mail rules. You can use the templates, for instance, to create a rule to play a sound when you receive a message from a particular person. To create one of these template-based rules, select the template and follow the steps in the wizard.

Creating an AutoReply (continued)

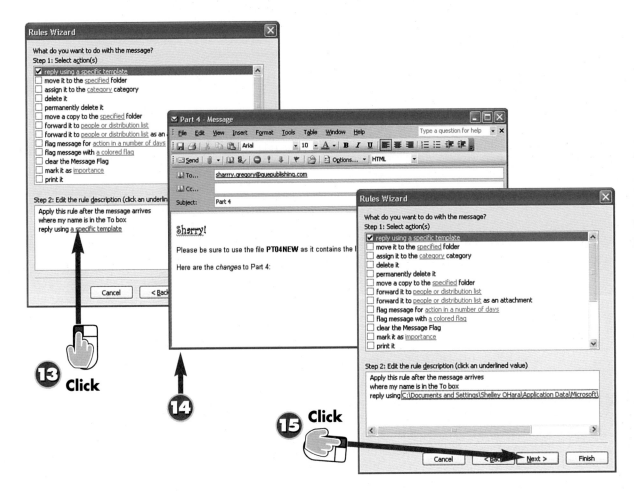

13 In the **Step 2** area, click the **A Specific Template** link to select the template (message) to use.

14 The Select Reply Template dialog box appears. Open the folder that contains the template you want to use, click the template to select it, and click **Open**.

15 The rule conditions and actions are listed. Click **Next**.

Changing Template Folders

If your template is not listed in the Select a Reply Template dialog box, display the Look In drop-down list and select **User Templates in File System**.

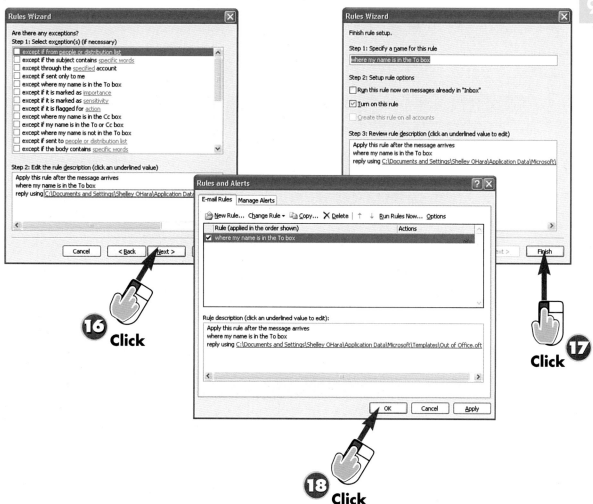

16 In the wizard screen that appears, you can click any of the various check boxes to specify any exceptions, but none are needed for the autoreply. Click **Next**.

17 Outlook displays the completed mail rule. Click **Finish**.

18 The new mail rule is listed in the Rules and Alerts dialog box. Click **OK**. Now, anyone who sends you a message will receive this reply.

End

Deleting a Rule
To delete a rule, click **Tools** and **Rules and Alerts**. You see the rules listed. Click the rule you want to delete and then click the **Delete** button.

Choosing Stationery

Start

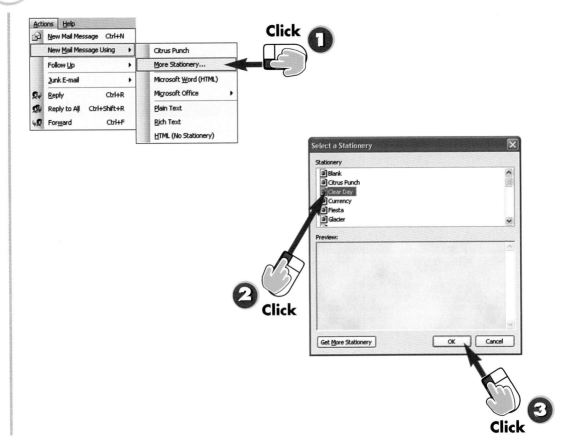

Click ①

② Click

③ Click

① Open the **Actions** menu, choose **New Mail Using**, and then select **More Stationery**.

② The Select a Stationery dialog box opens. In the **Stationery** list, click the stationery you want to use; a preview of the stationery appears in the **Preview** area.

③ When you find stationery that you like, click **OK**.

INTRODUCTION

If you want your e-mail messages to look more professional or fancy, you can use Outlook's Stationery feature. You can select any one of Outlook's predesigned message formats.

Making Your Stationery Choice Permanent
To configure Outlook to always use stationery, open the **Tools** menu and choose **Options**. The Options dialog box opens; click the **Mail Format** tab. Click the **down arrow** next to the **Use This Stationery by Default** field, and choose the stationery you want to use from the list that appears. When you're finished, click **OK**.

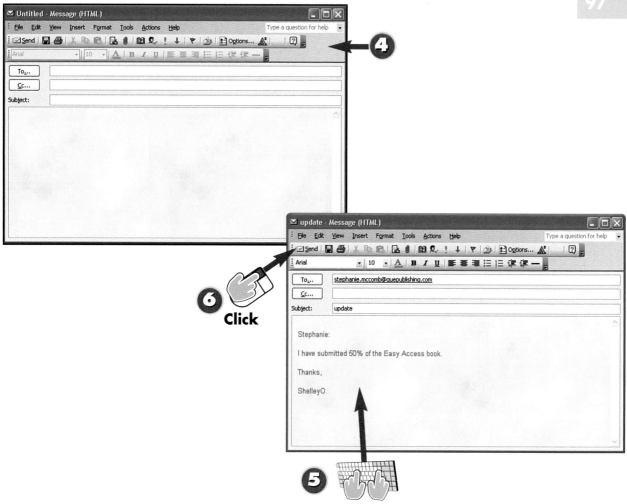

Click

(4) Outlook creates a new message with the stationery you selected.

(5) Just as you would in a regular e-mail message, complete the address information, type a subject, and type the message contents.

(6) Click the **Send** button to send the message.

End

Getting More Stationery
Click the **Get More Stationery** button in the Select a Stationery dialog box to install additional stationery from Microsoft's Web site. Alternatively, if you see an alert message notifying you that more stationery is available on the Office setup disks, you can insert the appropriate disk and install the additional stationery when prompted.

Setting a Default Stationery
If you want to use a particular stationery for all new messages, you can set it as the default. See the next task to learn how.

Selecting Your Default Stationery

Start

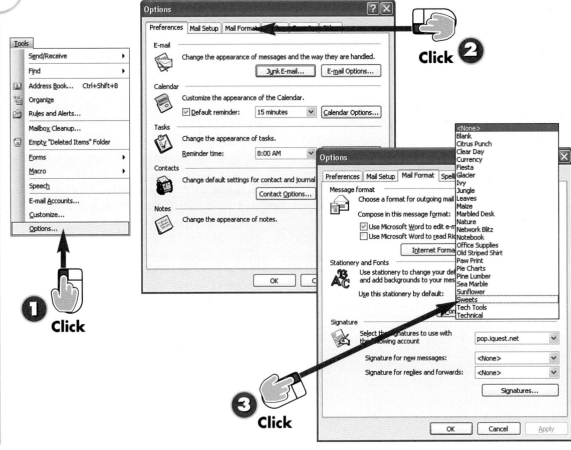

Click ②

① Click

③ Click

① Open the **Tools** menu and choose **Options**.

② The Options dialog box opens. Click the **Mail Format** tab.

③ Click the **down arrow** next to the **Use Stationery by Default** field and select the stationery you want to use.

If you like using stationery, you may want to set up Outlook to always use a particular stationery for all new messages. You can do so using the Mail Format options. Keep in mind that you can always change the stationery for individual messages.

Previewing Stationery
Because the drop-down list does not display a preview, it may be handy to click the **Stationery Picker** button and select from the various options to preview and select your stationery.

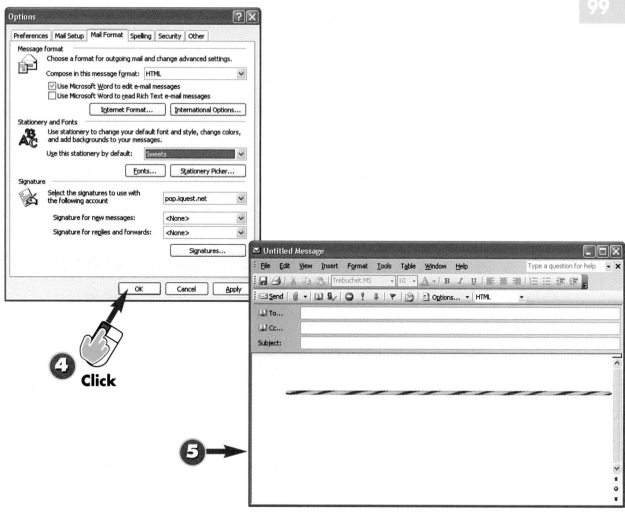

Click

The new default stationery is listed. Click **OK**.

When you create a new message, Outlook uses the stationery you selected.

End

Setting E-mail Options

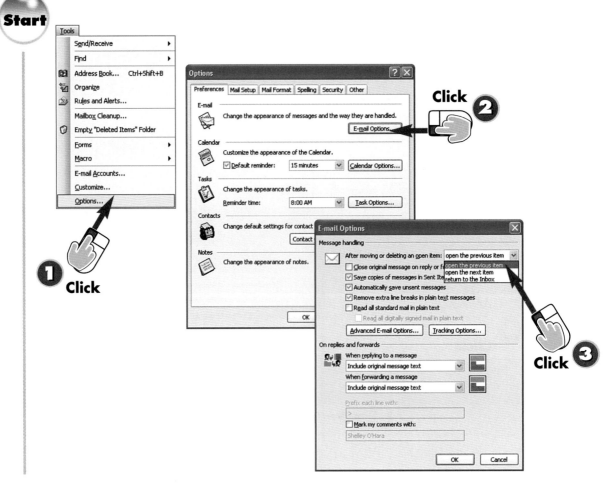

1 Open the **Tools** menu and choose **Options**.

2 The Options dialog box opens. Click the **E-mail Options** button to open the E-mail Options dialog box.

3 To specify which message to display after you move or delete an item, choose an option from the **After Moving or Deleting an Open Item** drop-down list.

You have many options for controlling how mail is created, sent, handled, and more. For example, you can specify whether, when you reply to a message, Outlook should include the text of the original message. You can also specify whether a copy of a sent message is stored in the Sent Items folder. You make these changes using the **E-mail Options** dialog box.

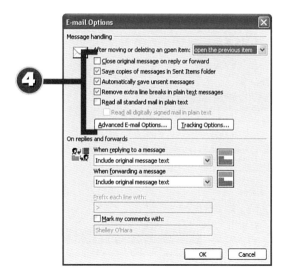

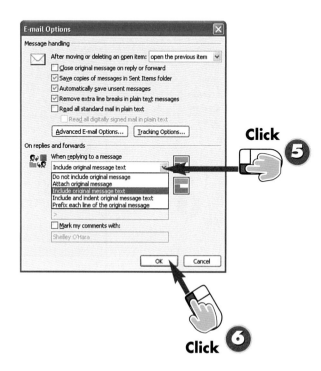

Click 5

Click 6

④ Enable or disable any additional message-handling options.

⑤ Using the drop-down lists in the **On Replies and Forwards** area, specify whether Outlook should include the original message text when you reply to or forward a message.

⑥ Click **OK** in the E-mail Options dialog box, and again in the Options dialog box.

End

Saving Copies of Sent Messages
By default, Outlook saves a copy of every e-mail message you send in the Sent Items folder. If you don't want a copy saved, uncheck the **Save Copies of Messages in Sent Items Folder** check box in the E-mail Options dialog box. You might do this if you don't need these copies or you don't want to take up the disk space required to store these messages.

Reply and Forward Options
For replies and forwarded messages, you can choose to attach the original text, to include and indent the text, or to add a prefix to each line of the original message or reply without including the original text.

Changing Your Mail Setup

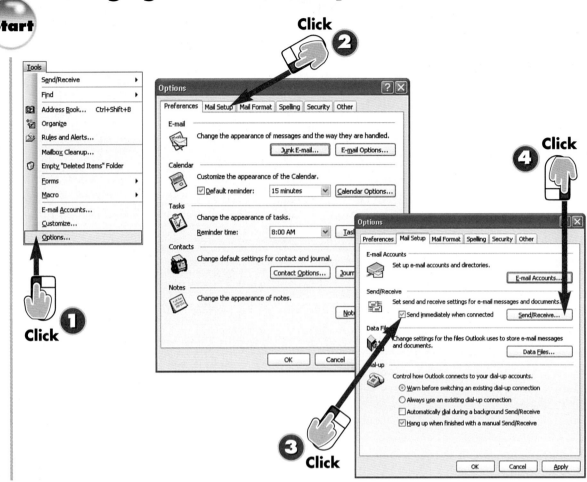

1. Open the **Tools** menu and choose **Options**.

2. The Options dialog box opens. Click the **Mail Setup** tab.

3. To send messages manually rather than automatically when you are connected to the Internet, uncheck the **Send Immediately When Connected** check box.

4. Click the **Send/Receive** button. The Send/Receive Groups dialog box opens.

If you click the **Send** button while connected to the Internet, Outlook immediately sends the message you created. You can, however, change Outlook's settings so that messages are sent manually. You make this change and adjust other related settings in the Mail Setup tab of Outlook's Options dialog box.

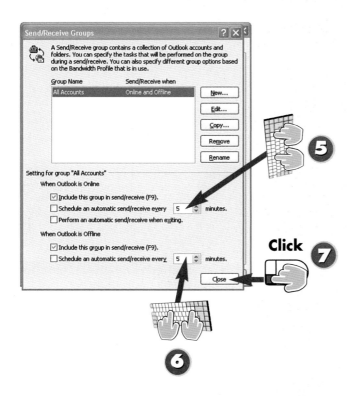

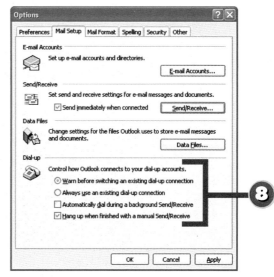

Click

5   To change how often Outlook checks for mail while you are online, mark the **Schedule an Automatic Send/Receive Every** check box in the **When Outlook Is Online** area and type a time (in minutes) into the spin box.

6   To set offline connection intervals in the **When Outlook Is Offline** section, mark the **Schedule an Automatic Send/Receive Every** check box type a time (in minutes) into the spin box.

7   Click **Close**.

8   To control how Outlook connects to your mail provider, choose the desired options in the **Dial-up** area of the Options dialog box. When you're finished, click **OK**.

End

Setting Up Multiple Mail Accounts

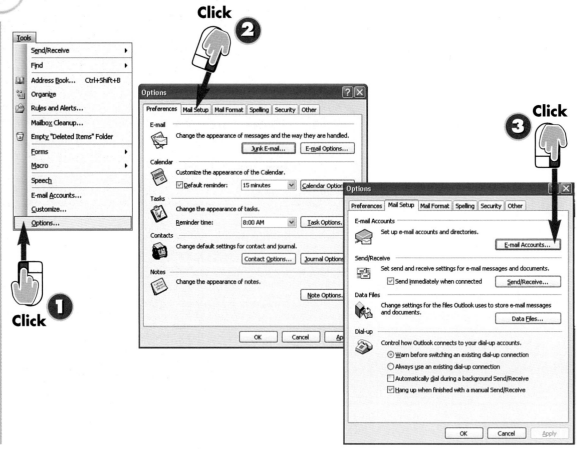

1. Open the **Tools** menu and choose **Options** to display the Options dialog box.

2. Click the **Mail Setup** tab.

3. The Mail Setup tab displays the options for setting up new mail accounts. Click the **E-mail Accounts** button to start the E-mail Accounts Wizard.

Setting Account Options

After additional accounts are set up, click the **Send/Receive** button on the Mail Setup tab of the Options dialog box to display the Send/Receive Groups dialog box. You can then specify how often each account is checked by selecting the mail account you want to customize and then choosing the appropriate options.

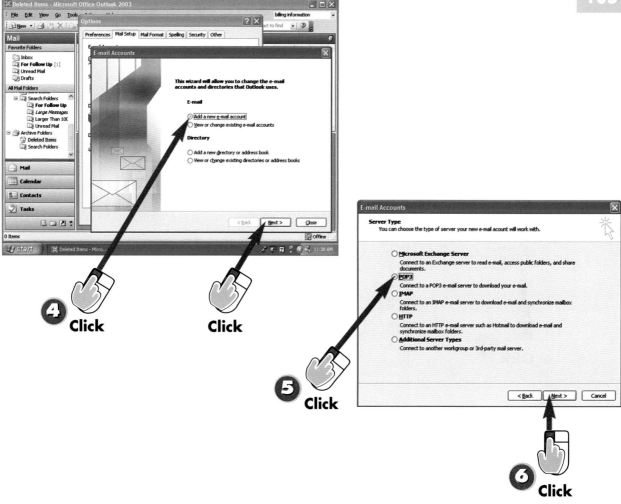

Click **4** **Click** **5** **Click** **6** **Click**

4 In the first screen of the E-mail Accounts Wizard, click the **Add a New E-mail Account** option button and click **Next**.

5 Click the option button next to the type of server that the new e-mail account will use (you can obtain this information from your e-mail provider), and click **Next**.

6 The next steps vary depending on your selection in step 5. Complete the steps on each screen, clicking **Next** to move from screen to screen and clicking **Finish** at the end of the setup process.

End

Server Types and Names
Your e-mail provider should give you the specific information about your e-mail account type, including the server types and names.

Completing the Wizard
As you learned in step 6, the specific steps in the E-mail Accounts Wizard vary depending on the server type you select in step 5. In general, though, you'll enter basic e-mail account information such as your name, e-mail address, server names, username, and password.

Setting the Default Mail Format

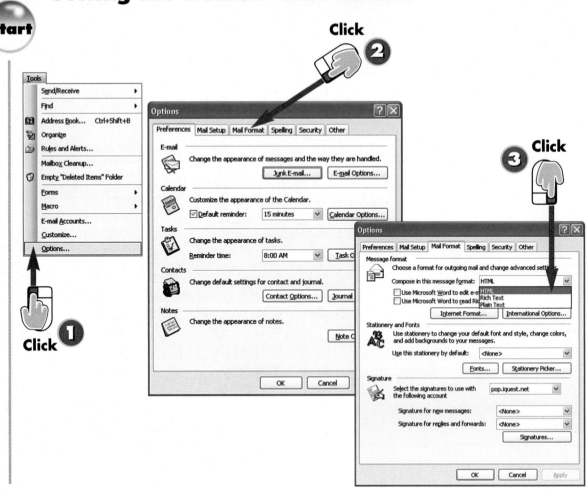

Start

Click ②

Click ③

Click ①

1. Open the **Tools** menu and choose **Options**.

2. The Options dialog box opens. Click the **Mail Format** tab.

3. To select a default format for new mail messages, click the **down arrow** next to the **Compose in This Message Format** field and select the format you want to use.

If you find that you constantly compose messages using Microsoft Word or some other message format, such as plain text, that is not Outlook's default setting, you can configure Outlook to use your preferred format by default.

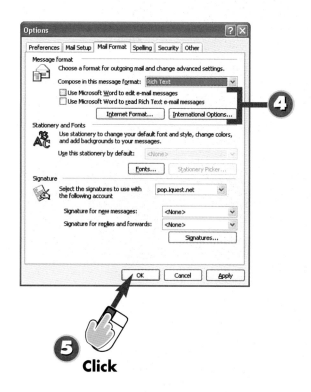

5 Click

4 To use Word to edit or read messages, check the **Use Microsoft Word to Edit E-mail Messages** and **Use Microsoft Word to Read Rich Text E-mail Messages** check boxes.

5 Click **OK**.

Changing the Default Font
To change the default font for new messages, replies, or forwarded messages, click the **Fonts** button in the Mail Format tab of the Options dialog box. Then, click the **Choose Font** button next to the message type whose font you want to change. Select the font, size, and style you want to use, and click **OK** once to close the Font dialog box, again to close the Fonts dialog box, and a third time to close the Options dialog box.

Creating an E-mail Signature

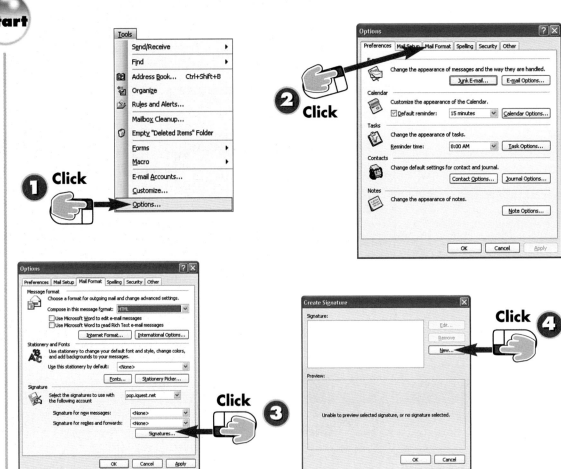

① Open the **Tools** menu and choose **Options**.

② The Options dialog box opens. Click the **Mail Format** tab.

③ Click the **Signatures** button.

④ The Create Signature dialog box opens. To create a new signature, click the **New** button.

If you frequently sign your messages using not only your name, but also additional information such as your job title and contact information, you'll appreciate Outlook's Signature feature. When enabled, it appends text of your choosing to the end of every message you create and/or reply to.

Using a Template

If you like, you can use a predesigned template for your signature. To do so, click the **Use This File as a Template** option button in the Create New Signature dialog box (see step 5), and then click the **Browse** button. In the dialog box that appears, locate the file you want to use, click it to select it, and click **Select**.

Click

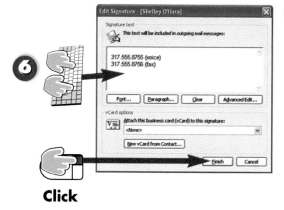

Click

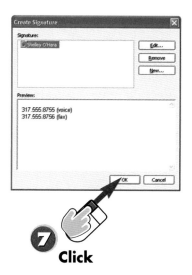

7 **Click**

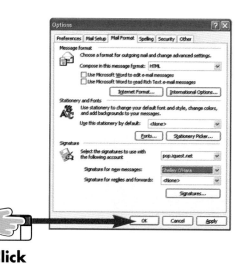

8 **Click**

5 Type your name as you want it to appear in your messages and click **Next**.

6 Type any additional text you want to include, such as your title, company, or contact information, and then click **Finish**.

7 A preview of your new signature appears in the Preview area of the Create Signature dialog box. If you are satisfied, click **OK**.

8 Your signature is selected as the default for new messages. Click **OK** to confirm the use of this signature.

End

Using a vCard

A *vCard* is a virtual business card that is recognized and supported by many contact programs. You can create a vCard and attach it to your messages by clicking the **New vCard from Contact** button in the Edit Signature dialog box (see step 6) and then completing the requested information to add the vCard to your Address Book. (See Part 5 for information on using your Address Book.) When you attach a vCard to your messages, the recipient can then easily add your information to his or her contact program.

Changing the Font

To change your signature's font, click the **Font** button in the Edit Signature dialog box (see step 6) . In the dialog box that appears, select the font, size, and style you want to use, and click **OK**.

Setting Deleted Items, Archived Folders, and Other E-mail Options

Start

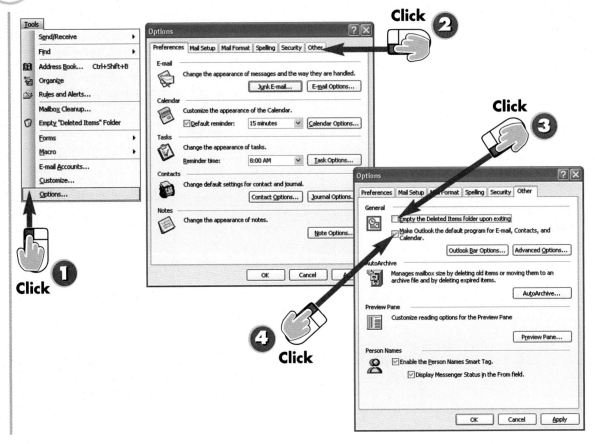

---

1 Open the **Tools** menu and choose **Options**.

2 The Options dialog box opens. Click the **Other** tab.

3 If you don't want to empty your Deleted Items folder manually, check the **Empty the Deleted Items Folder upon Exiting** check box.

4 To make Outlook your default mail program (rather than any other mail programs installed on your computer), check the **Make Outlook the Default Program...** check box.

You can view and change still more settings using the Other tab in the Options dialog box. This tab enables you to set a hodge-podge of options, including whether items you delete remain in your Deleted Items folder until you manually empty it, which program is your default mail program, and when messages are archived.

TIP

Disabling the Person Name SmartTag
When you type a name in an e-mail message's To field, Outlook checks your contact list and displays any matching names. You can press **Enter** to select the name rather than type it completely. If you do not want to use this feature, you can turn it off by unchecking the **Enable the Person Names Smart Tag** check box in the Other tab of the Options dialog box.

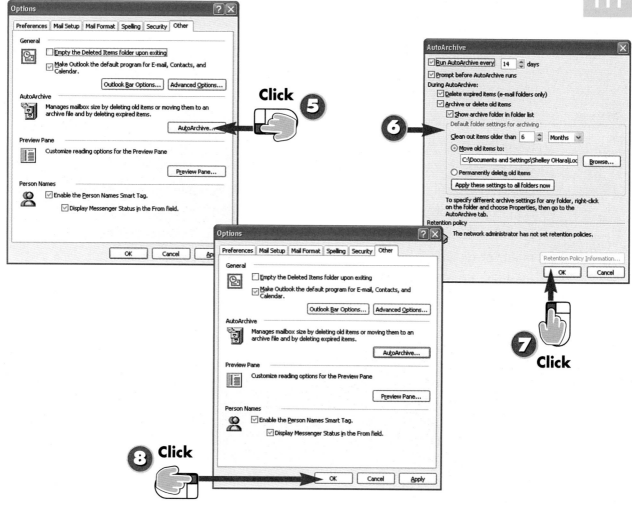

5 To view or change the settings for automatic archiving, click the **AutoArchive** button to open the AutoArchive dialog box.

6 Select how often the archive is made, whether you are prompted to run the archive, and what happens during the archive.

7 Click **OK** to close the AutoArchive dialog box.

8 Click **OK** to close the Options dialog box.

End

Archive Options
Outlook prompts you before running AutoArchive, and does so every 14 days. You can choose whether to run the archive at that time. Outlook archives items older than six months, but you can change this interval as well.

Customizing the Preview Pane
To customize how messages in the Preview pane behave, click the **Preview Pane** button on the Options dialog box's Other tab. In the dialog box that appears, you can, among other things, mark an item displayed in the Preview pane as "read" after so many seconds. Make your changes and click **OK** to return to the Options dialog box.

Organizing Contacts

During the course of your day, you probably have contact with many people, including business contacts, co-workers, family, friends, colleagues, customers, and others. For each individual, you need to know key information, such as the contact's e-mail address, phone number, mailing address, fax number, and so on. To help you keep track of all this information, you can use Outlook's Contacts feature. With this feature, you can create contact records with as much or as little information as you need for that particular contact. This part explains how to organize contact information.

Contacts Window

current view   menubar   toolbar

task pane →

contact list

Outlook bar →

Contacts button   Status bar

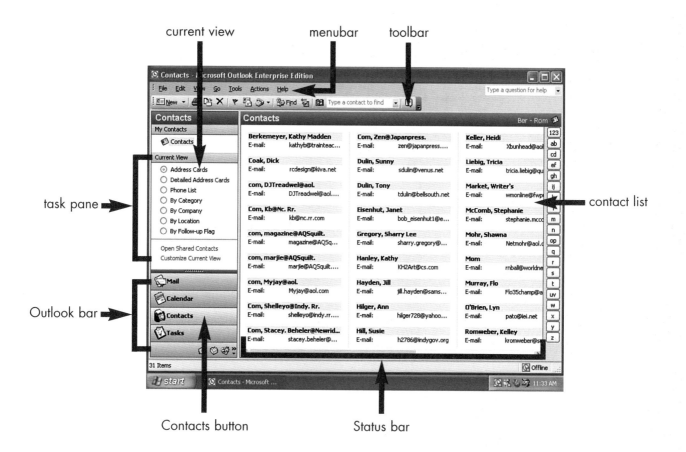

Viewing the Contacts Window

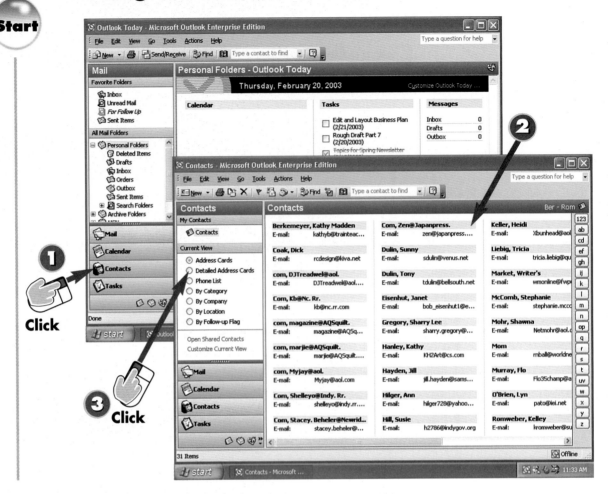

1. Click the **Contacts** button in the Outlook Bar.

2. A list of contacts you have entered appears. By default, the list displays both the mailing and e-mail address of each contact (unless no mailing address has been entered).

3. To change how your contacts are displayed in the list, click one of the view options in the **Current View** area of the Outlook task bar.

INTRODUCTION

To keep track of clients, vendors, friends, family, co-workers, and others, you can use Outlook's Contacts feature. You most often use Contacts to quickly enter an e-mail address, but the Contacts feature also is useful for entering traditional contact information such as street addresses, phone numbers, fax numbers, and so on. In this task, take some time to explore the Contacts window.

TIP

Adding Contacts
You'll learn how to add contacts in the next task.

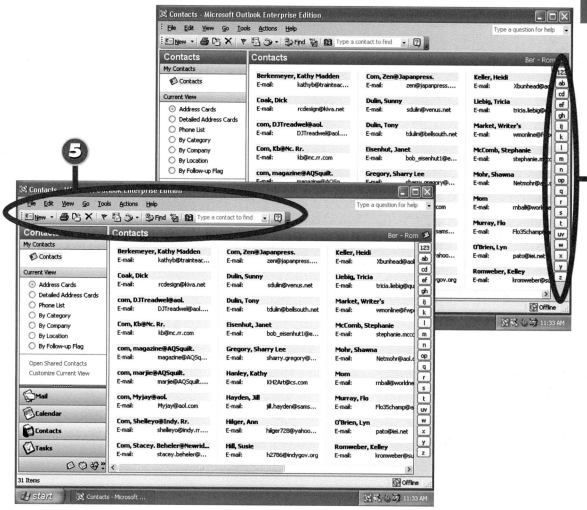

④ Click any of the buttons on the right side of your screen to quickly display a set of contacts, such as contacts whose last names start with the letter *S*.

⑤ The toolbar includes buttons for creating and managing contacts.

End

Exiting Outlook
To exit Outlook, click the **Close** button in the Outlook window, or open the **File** menu and choose **Exit**.

Adding a New Contact

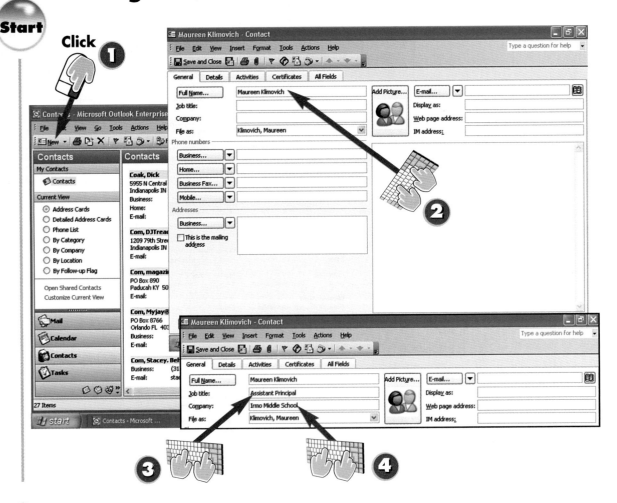

1. In the main Outlook toolbar, click the **New** button.

2. Type your contact's full name into the **Full Name** field. Outlook uses this name for the **File As** field.

3. Click in the **Job Title** field and type your contact's job title.

4. Type the name of the company where your contact works into the **Company** field.

TIP

Navigating the Contact Window
Rather than clicking in each field before typing in it, you can press the **Tab** key on your keyboard to move from field to field in the Contact window.

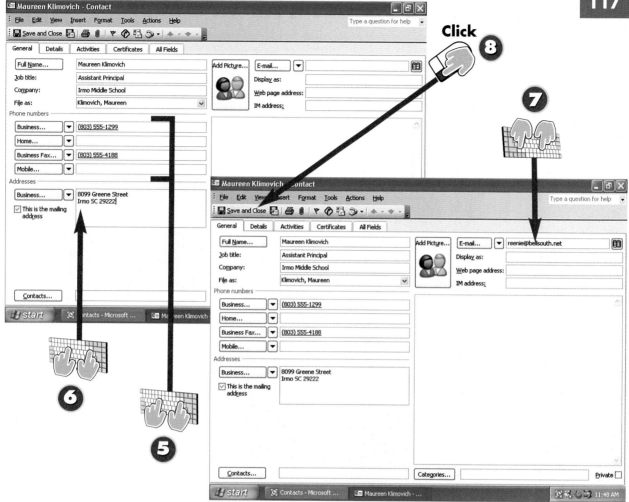

Click

5 Type your contact's various phone numbers into the **Business**, **Home**, **Business Fax**, and **Mobile** fields.

6 Type the contact's mailing address into the **Addresses** area. If this is the mailing address, check that text box.

7 Click the **E-mail** field and type the contact's e-mail address.

8 Click the **Save and Close** button to create the new contact.

End

Adding Other Information

You can also type your contact's Web page address, IM address, and any notes about the contact in the General tab of the Contact window.

Customizing Fields

Some fields in the Contact window, such as the ones in the Phone Numbers and Addresses areas, are preceded by down-arrow buttons. Click any of these buttons to reveal a drop-down list of other field options. For example, you can click the **down-arrow** button next to the Business field in the Addresses section and choose **Home** from the list that appears; then you can enter the contact's home address in the field. To again view the business address, simply click the **down-arrow** again and choose **Business** from the list. For more information about customizing fields, see the task "Customizing Contact Fields" later in this part.

Adding a Contact from an E-mail

Start

2 Click

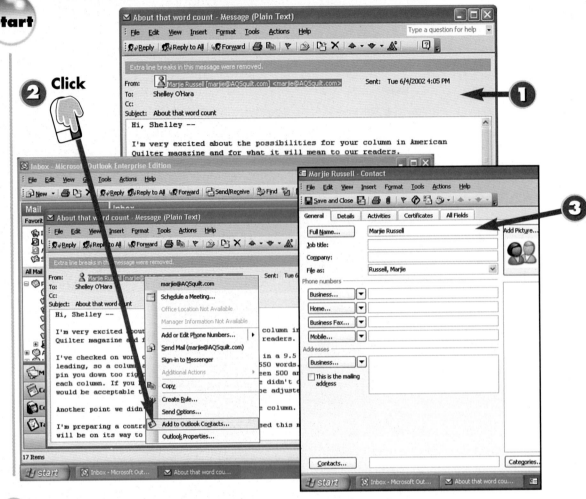

1 Open an e-mail to or from the person you want to add to your contact list.

2 Right-click the sender's name in the message header and then click **Add to Outlook Contacts** in the shortcut menu that appears.

3 A contact window opens, with the **Full Name**, **File As**, and **E-mail** fields already completed.

If you've sent or received an e-mail message from a person whom you'd like to add to your contact list, you can use that message to create the new contact.

TIP

Contact Already Entered?
If the contact has already been entered in your contact list, the shortcut menu shown in step 2 will feature a command for opening the Contact window. Do so, make changes to the information as needed, and click the **Save and Close** button when you are finished.

Click 5

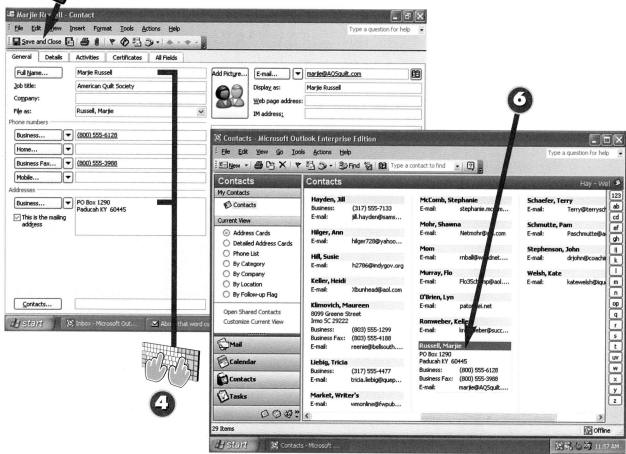

4

4 Type information about your contact into any fields as needed.

5 When the entry is complete, click the **Save and Close** button in the main Outlook toolbar.

6 The contact is added to your contact list.

End

Other Shortcut Commands
You can select other commands from the shortcut menu shown in step 2, including ones that enable you to schedule a meeting or send mail.

Opening and Editing an Existing Contact

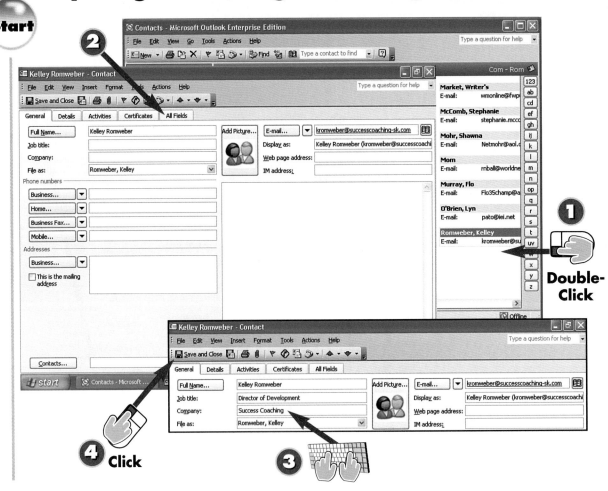

Double-Click

Click

1 Locate the contact you want to open in your contact list, and double-click it.

2 The Contact window opens, displaying information about the contact.

3 Click in a field and type or edit the information.

4 When you finish viewing or editing the contact information, click the **Save and Close** button in the Contact window's toolbar.

Start

End

INTRODUCTION

When you want to view the information you have entered about a contact, you can do so. For example, you might want to add to or edit the information. Or you might need to refer any notes or activities for the contact before making a phone call.

TIP

Locating a Contact
For help locating the contact you want to open, see the tasks "Scrolling Through Contacts" and "Searching for a Contact" later in this part.

TIP

Displaying Additional Contacts
You can move from one contact record to the next by clicking the **Previous Item** (up arrow) and **Next Item** (down arrow) buttons in the Contact window's toolbar.

Adding a Picture

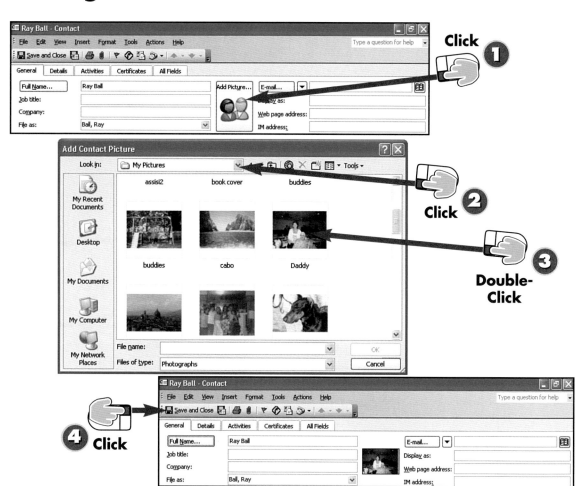

1 After you've created a new contact or opened an existing one, click the **Add Picture** button in the Contact window's General tab.

2 The Add Contact Picture dialog box opens. Open the drive and folder that contains the image you want to add.

3 Double-click the picture file to add it to the Contact window. The picture is added.

4 Click the **Save and Close** button to update the contact record.

End

INTRODUCTION

Suppose you manage a large department or team. To match the names of your employees with their faces, you can add a picture to each person's contact information. Alternatively, you might add pictures of your family and friends just for fun.

TIP

Opening Drives and Folders
In the Add Contact Picture dialog box, locate the drive and folder that contains the photo you want by clicking the **down-arrow** next to the **Look In** field, by clicking the **Up One Level** button, by clicking any of the folders in the Places bar, or by double-clicking any of the folders in the folders list.

Entering Detailed Contact Information

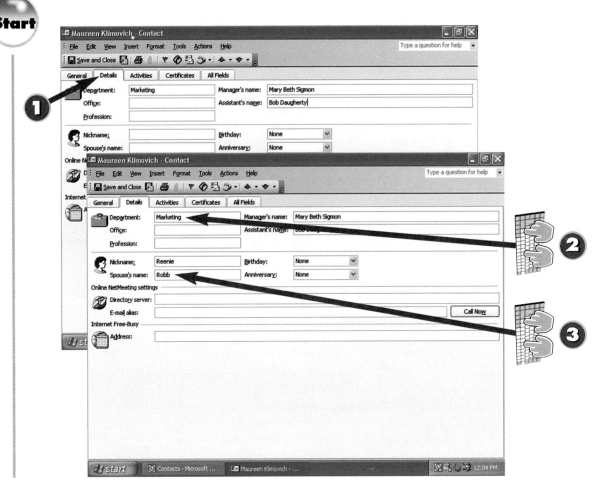

After you've created a new contact or opened an existing one, click the **Details** tab in the Contact window.

Type professional information about the contact, such as his or her department, office, profession, manager's name, and assistant's name.

Enter any personal information about the contact, such as his or her nickname and the name of his or her spouse.

If you use Outlook simply to send and receive e-mail, you may not want to bother completing all the available fields in the Contact window. On the other hand, if you use Outlook as a contact manager, you should take a look at all the types of information you can store about each contact.

Entering Contacts from the Same Company

If several of your contacts work for the same company, you can use a shortcut to enter the company information when creating new contacts. To do so, open a Contact window that already contains the company information. Then, in the Contact window's menu bar, choose **Actions**, **New Contact from Same Company**. Outlook will create a new record but complete the company information for you.

Click 5

Click 4

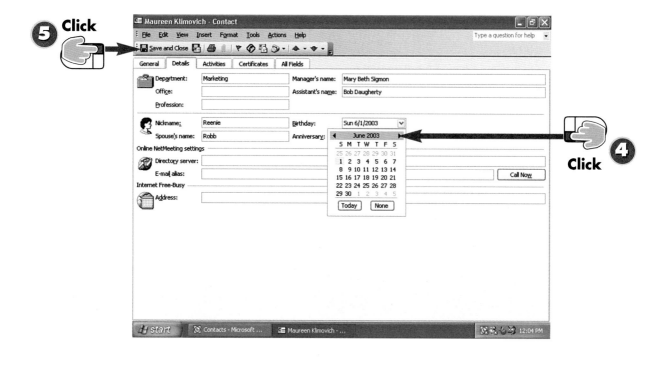

4. Type the contact's birthday and anniversary in the appropriate field, or click the **down-arrow** button next to the field and use the minicalendar to locate the date.

5. Click **Save and Close** to close the contact window.

End

Using Other Tabs

TIP

You can use the Activities tab to track a contact's activities (see "Journaling Activities for a Contact" later in this task for more information) . Use the Certificates tab to set up security options for encrypted messages, and use All Fields to create a customized tab listing the fields you want to include on the tab. You can select which fields to include from a drop-down list.

Assigning a Category to a Contact

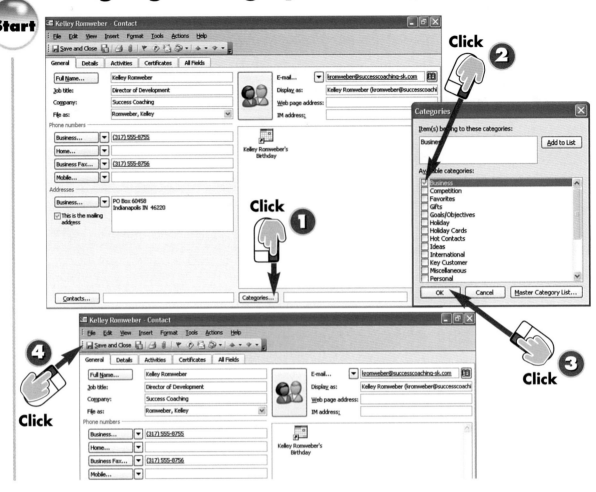

1. After you've created a new contact or opened an existing one, click the **Categories** button at the bottom of the Contact window's General tab.

2. A list of available categories appears; click the check box next to the category you want to assign to select it.

3. Click **OK**.

4. The category is listed on the General tab; click the **Save and Close** button.

End

Customizing Contact Fields

Start

Click 4

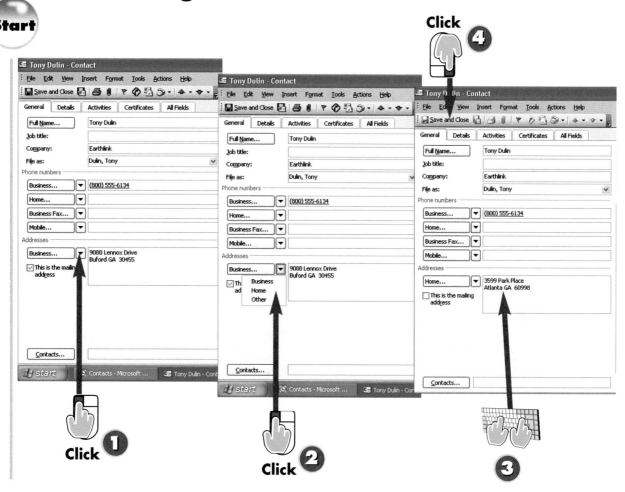

Click 1

Click 2

3

1. After you create a new contact or open an existing one, click the **down-arrow** next to the field you want to customize.

2. Select a different field-name option from the list that appears.

3. The field name is changed. Type any needed information into the newly named field (here, the contact's home address).

4. Click the **Save and Close** button.

End

INTRODUCTION

Outlook doesn't limit you to using the fields that appear in the Contact window by default. Some fields, such as the ones in the Phone Numbers and Addresses areas, are preceded by down-arrow buttons, indicating that they are customizable. For example, you can click the **down-arrow** button next to the Business field in the Addresses section and choose **Home** from the list that appears, and then enter the contact's home address in the field. To again view the contact's business address, simply click the **down-arrow** again and choose **Business** from the list.

TIP

Viewing Fields

Suppose you've entered a home address as well as a business address for a contact. You can quickly view both addresses by clicking the **All Fields** tab in the Contact window. Then, click the **down-arrow** next to the **Select From** field and choose **Address Fields** from the list that appears. You can make changes to both addresses as needed from this tab.

Flagging a Contact for Follow-Up

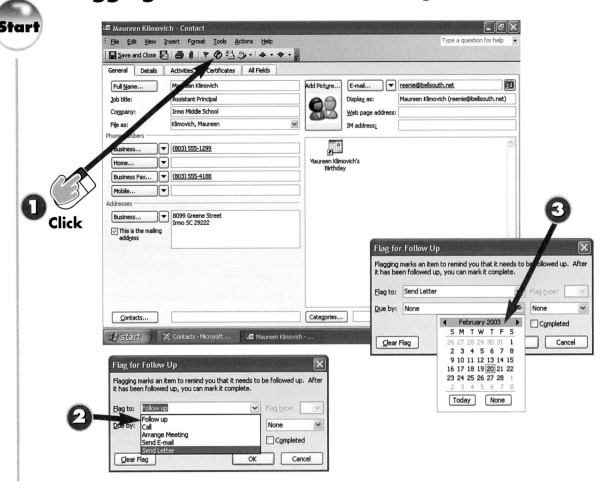

Start

① Click

②

③

1. After you create a new contact or open an existing one that requires follow-up, click the **Follow Up** button in the Contact window.

2. Click the **down-arrow** next to the **Flag To** field and choose **Follow Up**, **Call**, **Arrange Meeting**, **Send E-mail**, or **Send Letter**.

3. Type a due date for the action in the **Due By** field, or click the **down-arrow** next to the field and use the minicalendar to locate the date.

To help you remember which of your contacts are expecting some sort of action from you, whether it's placing a phone call or sending an information packet, you can flag those contacts with whom you need to follow up. Then you can see at a glance which of your contacts require your attention.

A Shortcut

TIP

If you prefer, simply click—rather than open—the contact you want to flag for follow-up in the contact list, and then click the **Follow Up** button on the main Outlook toolbar.

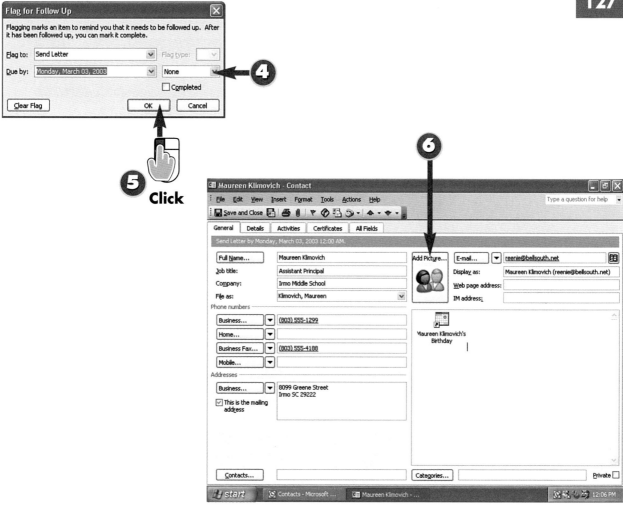

4 If the action should be performed before a particular time on the due date, type the time into the field next to the **Due By** field (the default is **None**) .

5 Click **OK**.

6 The flag is noted on the Contact window, as well as in the contact list.

End

Marking the Activity as Complete
If you want to keep the flag but indicate that the activity was completed, click the flag and then select **Completed** from the list that appears. Alternatively, remove the flag by clicking it and selecting **Normal** from the list that appears.

Viewing Flagged Contacts
To view all flagged contacts on one screen, click the **By Follow-up Flag** option button in the Current View area of the Contacts Task pane. (To learn more, see the task "Changing the Contacts View.")

Deleting a Contact

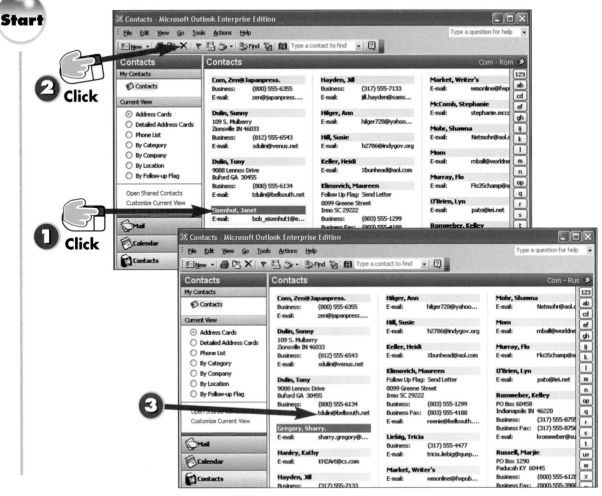

1. In the contact list, select the contact that you want to delete.

2. Click the **Delete** button in the main Outlook toolbar.

3. The contact is deleted.

TIP

Undoing the Deletion
Outlook does not prompt you to confirm the deletion. If you delete a contact by mistake, open the **Edit** menu and choose **Undo** to undo the deletion. Alternatively, retrieve the item from the Deleted Items folder (see "Undeleting an Item" in Part 3, "Reading and Handling E-mail Messages").

Changing the Contacts View

Start

① Click

② Click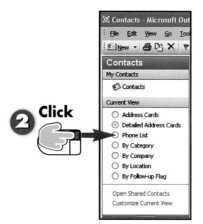

③ Click

④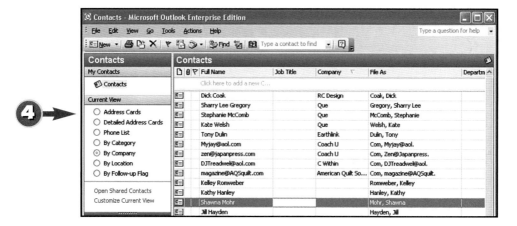

① To view more detailed information about each contact in your list, click the **Detailed Address Cards** option button in the **Current View** area of the Contacts Task pane.

② The contact list now displays more detailed information about each contact. To display your contacts as a phone list in table format, click the **Phone List** option button.

③ The phone numbers of each contact now appear. Click **By Category**, **By Company**, **By Location**, or **By Follow-Up Flag** to group your contacts.

④ The contacts are grouped according to the criterion you selected (here, **By Company**).

End

INTRODUCTION

When you first open Outlook's Contacts feature, the Contacts window opens in Address view, which displays both the e-mail and mailing address of each contact You can change the view to see your contact list in another

TIP

Using the View Menu
If you prefer, you can use the View menu to arrange your contacts. Click **View**, **Arrange By**, and select the grouping you want.

TIP

Sorting by Using Column Headings
In the Phone List and Group By views, you can sort contacts using any of the available columns. For example, to sort the entries in your phone list by company, click the **Company** column heading.

Printing Contact Information

Start

Click

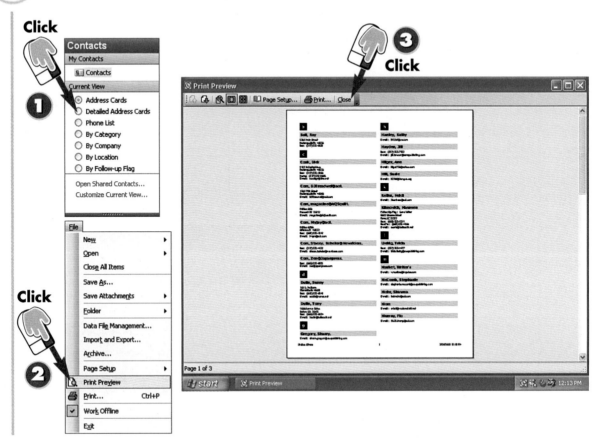

Click ③

Click ②

1. Depending on what you want to print, choose the appropriate view (here, **Detailed Address Card**) from the **Current View** area of the Contacts Task pane.

2. If you want to see how the printout will look before you print it, open the **File** menu and choose **Print Preview.**

3. When you are finished previewing the printout, click the **Close** button.

There may be times when you want to print contact information—for example, if you plan to travel without your laptop. You might print a company phone list or a list of customers with address and contact information for sales calls. Outlook lets you print contact information based on any of the available views.

TIP

Setting Up the Page
You can fine-tune your printout by using the Page Setup options, which vary depending on the current view. To open the Page Setup dialog box, click the **Page Setup** button in the Print Preview window, or open the **File** menu and choose **Page Setup**. Select the style to modify, make changes as needed, and click **OK**.

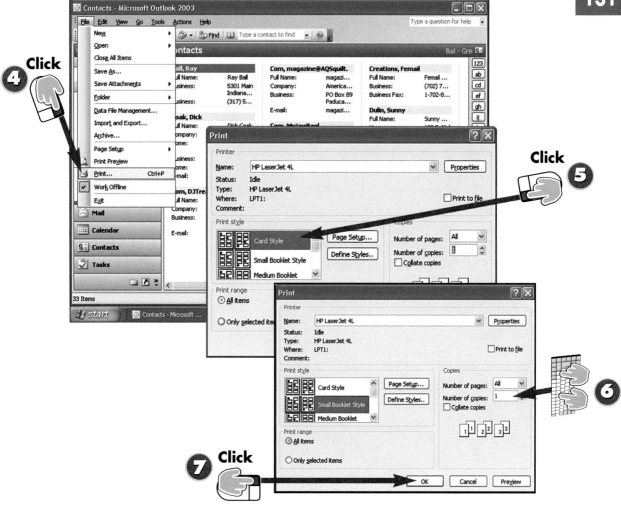

Click 4

Click 5

 6

Click 7

4 To print the contact information, open the **File** menu and choose **Print**.

5 The print options vary depending on the current view. For example, in Detailed Address Cards view, you can select from several print styles. Change your options as needed.

6 Type in the number of copies you want to print.

7 Click **OK**. The contact list is printed.

End

Print One Contact
TIP To print a single contact, display that contact on-screen. Then select **File**, **Print** and click **OK**.

Shortcut
TIP If you're confident your printout will turn out fine, print it directly from the contact list by clicking the **Print** button on the main Outlook toolbar. Alternatively, press **Ctrl+P**.

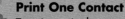

Scrolling Through Contacts

Start

Click **1**

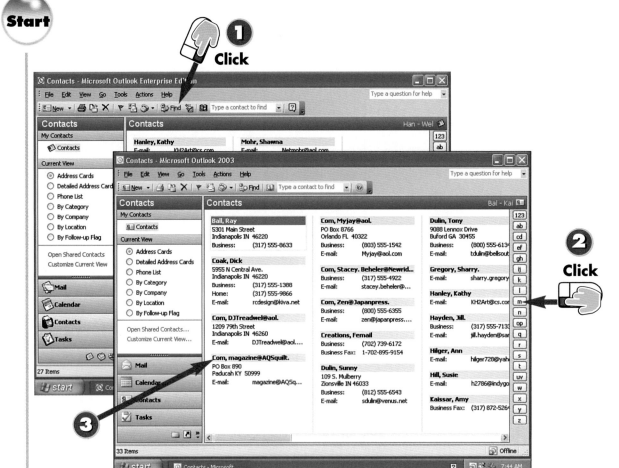

2

Click

1 The default view lists names alphabetical.

2 To quickly scroll to a contact, click the starting letter of that person's last name.

3 The first contact that starts with the selected letter is highlighted onscreen.

End

INTRODUCTION

When you display your contacts in Address Card or Detailed Address Card view, Outlook displays as many contacts as will fit in the current window. In those views, you can click any of the buttons on the right side of your screen to quickly display a specific set of contacts, such as those whose last names start with the letter M. These buttons act much like the tabs you find on paper-based address books.

TIP

Scrolling Through Columns
In the Phone List and Group By views, you can see as many columns as will fit onscreen. To view additional columns, click the scroll arrows along the bottom and right side of the window.

Searching for a Contact

Start

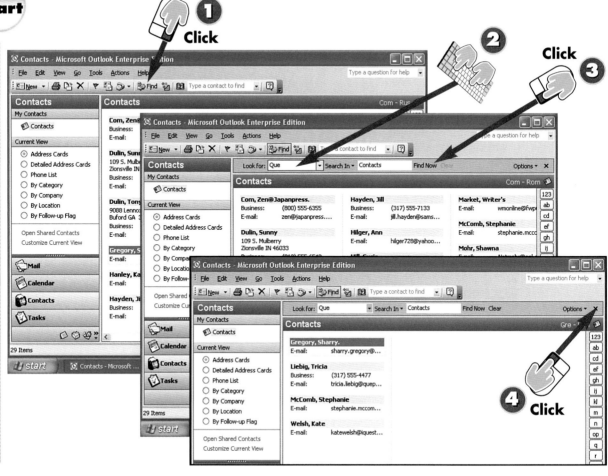

Click ①

Click ② ③

④ **Click**

① Click the **Find** button in the main Outlook toolbar.

② The Find bar opens. In the **Look For** text box, type the contact's name in part or in full, or any other information about the contact, such as the company he or she works for.

③ Click the **Find Now** button.

④ Outlook displays in the contact list only those contacts that match your search criteria. To close the search results, click the Find bar's **Close** button.

End

INTRODUCTION

Scrolling through the list to find a particular contact can be tedious. Instead, you can search for a contact. You might also search if you can't remember the name of your contact but do remember some other detail. You can search on any field.

TIP

Opening Matched Items
You open contacts that match your search criteria just as you do any other contacts in a contact list: by double-clicking them.

TIP

Setting Search Options
Change the search options by clicking the Find bar's **Options** button and then clicking **Advanced Find**. You can select to search based on category, e-mail address, or other entries. Make your choices and click **Find Now**.

Sending an E-mail to a Contact

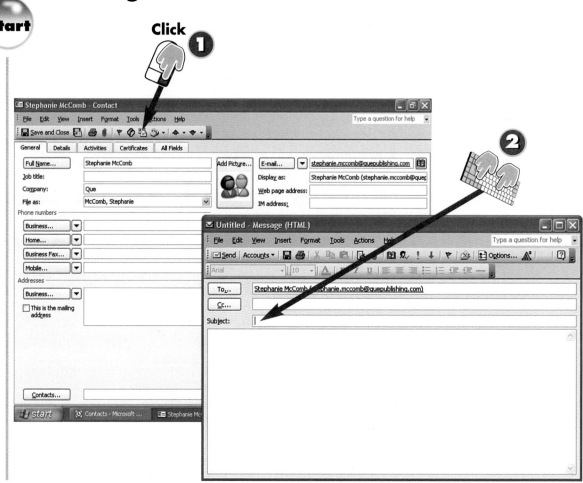

Start

Click

1 After you create a new contact or open an existing one to whom you want to send an e-mail message, click the **New Message to Contact** button in the Contact window.

2 An Untitled Message window opens with the selected contact's e-mail address entered in the To field. Type a subject for the message into the **Subject** field.

Click

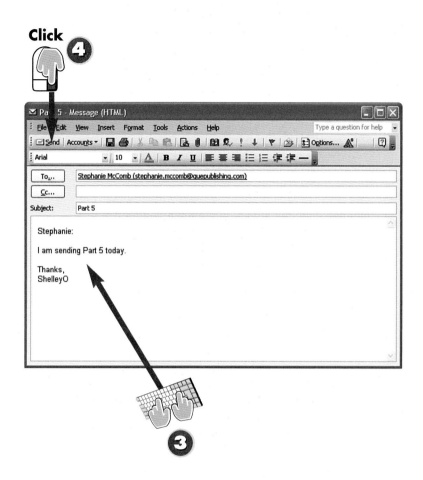

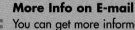

3 Click in the message area and type the contents of the message.

4 Click the **Send** button. Assuming you are online and have set up Outlook to automatically send your messages, the message will be sent.

More Info on E-mail

TIP

You can get more information about sending e-mail in Part 2, "Creating E-mail Messages."

Calling a Contact

Start

Click 1

Click 2

Click 3

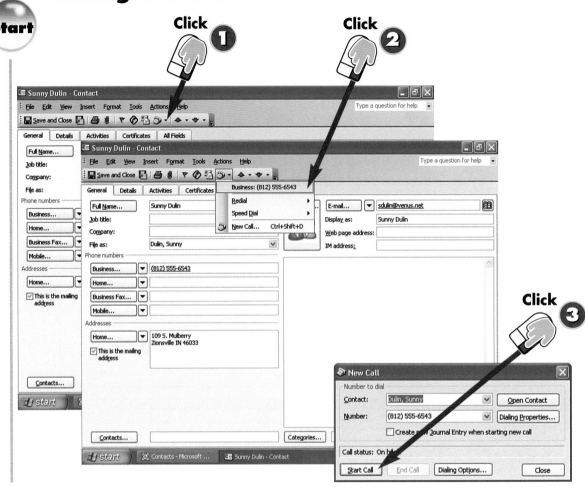

1 After you create a new contact or open an existing one you want to call, click the **down-arrow** next to the **AutoDialer** button.

2 A list containing the contact's phone numbers appears; select the number you want to dial.

3 The New Call dialog box opens with the selected number entered. Click the **Start Call** button.

If your telephone is hooked up to your computer, you can use Outlook to dial a contact's phone number and connect the call. When the call goes through, you simply pick up your phone's receiver and talk.

A Shortcut

TIP

If you prefer, simply click—rather than open—the contact you want to call in the contact list, and then click the **down-arrow** next to the **AutoDialer** button to select the desired phone number.

Dialing the Default Number

TIP

To dial the contact's default number (the first number listed, which, in the standard list, is the business number), simply click the **AutoDialer** button rather than clicking the **down-arrow** next to it.

Click 5

Click 6

4 Outlook dials the number. When prompted, pick up your telephone receiver and click **Talk**.

5 Click **End Call** when the call is complete.

6 Click **Close** to close the New Call dialog box.

End

Only One Number?
TIP If you have entered only one number for a contact, only that number is listed. If you have entered several, you can select which number to dial from the **AutoDialer drop-down** list.

Redialing
TIP To redial a previously dialed number, click **Redial** in the AutoDialer drop-down list shown in step 2, and then select the desired number from the list that appears. You can also set up and dial using speed-dial; consult Outlook's online help for speed-dial instructions.

Sending a Letter to a Contact

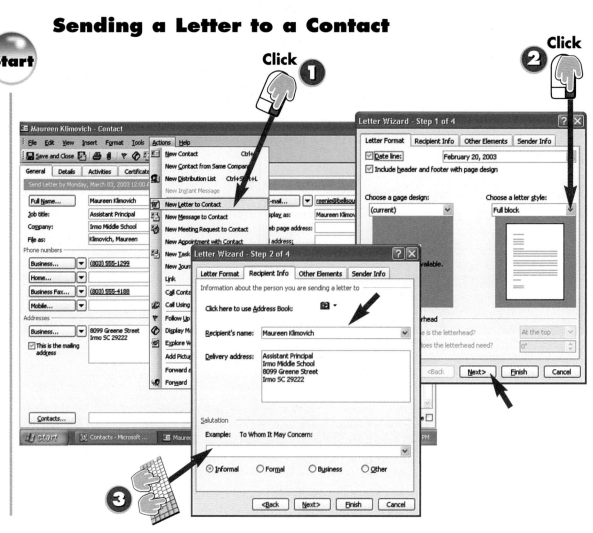

Start

Click ①

Click ②

③

①   After you create a new contact or open an existing one to whom you want to send a letter, open the **Actions** menu and choose **New Letter to Contact**.

②   Word's Letter wizard starts. Select a page design and letter style, and click **Next**.

③   The contact's name and address are pulled from the contact list and inserted in the **Recipient's Name** and **Delivery Address** fields. Type a salutation and click **Next**.

If you want to send a letter to a contact whose address information has been entered into Outlook, you don't need to look up the address and then type it into a document. Instead, you can create a letter, complete with the address information, from within Outlook. This feature uses Word's Letter wizard; after using Outlook to create the letter, you type, save, and print the letter from within Word. Note that to use this feature you must have Word installed on your computer.

Skipping to the End

TIP

You can skip steps in Word's Letter wizard and accept the default settings by clicking the **Finish** button.

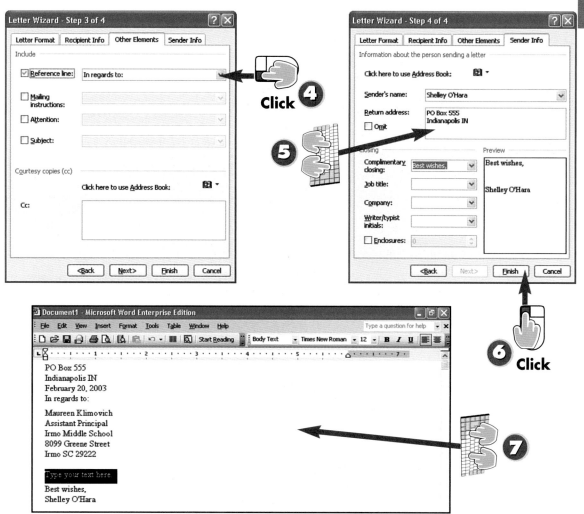

4 Select any other elements you want to include in your letter (a reference line, mailing instructions, attention, subject, or cc entries) and click **Next**.

5 Complete the sender information, including your name, address, and closing, if needed.

6 Click **Finish**.

7 A Word window opens with your letter displayed. Type the letter. (Consult Word's online help or *Easy Microsoft Word 11* for complete instructions on typing, formatting, and printing a letter.)

End

TIP

Performing a Mail Merge
You can use your contact list to create a mail-merge letter in Word. Consult your Office manual for instructions.

TIP

Printing Envelopes
To print an envelope, use Word's handy **Tools**, **Envelopes and Labels** command. Again, consult Word's Help system or *Easy Microsoft Word 11* for complete details on using this program.

Scheduling an Appointment with a Contact

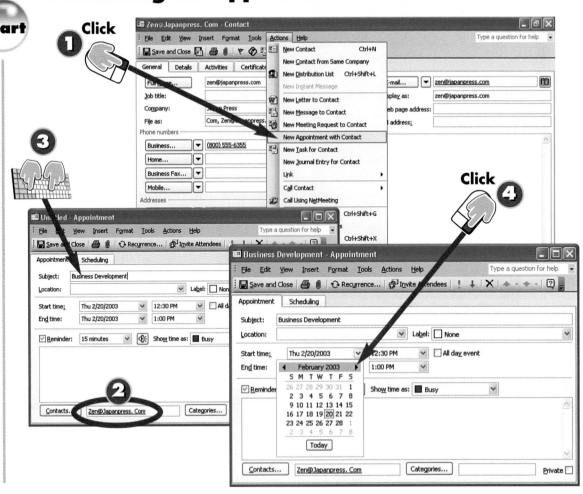

1 Open the contact and then open the **Actions** menu and choose **New Appointment with Contact**.

2 The Appointment window opens with the selected contact listed in the Contacts field.

3 In the **Subject** field, type a name for the appointment. This text will appear on the calendar and in the title bar of the Appointment window.

4 Type the appointment's date in the **Start Time** field or click the **down-arrow** next to the field and use the minicalendar to select the date.

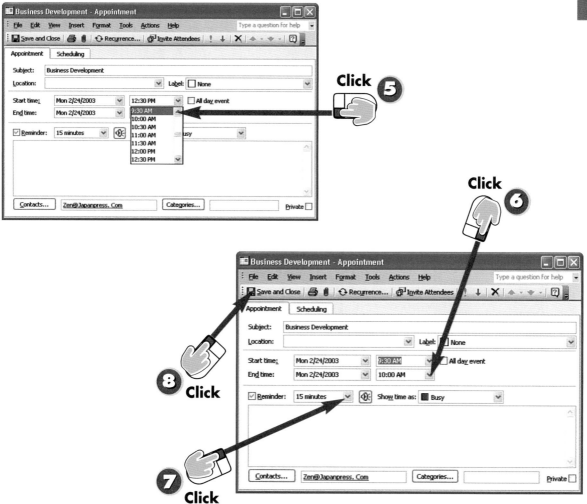

Click **5**

Click **6**

8 Click

7 Click

5 Type the appointment's start time or click the **down-arrow** and choose the start time from the drop-down list.

6 By default, appointments last for 30 minutes. To change the end time, type the correct time into the **End Time** field, or use the field's drop-down list to choose a new time.

7 Outlook displays reminders 15 minutes before appointments are to begin. To change the lead time, choose a time from the **Reminder** drop-down list.

8 Click the **Save and Close** button in the Contact window's toolbar to schedule the appointment.

End

Multiday Events
If the appointment will span multiple days, type the appointment's end date into the **End Time** field or click the **down-arrow** next to the field and use the minicalendar to select the date.

Scheduling a Meeting
You can schedule a meeting from within a Contact window using the same basic steps as the ones shown here; simply choose **New Meeting Request to Contact** from the **Action** menu in step 2.

Creating a Task
You can create task items related to a contact from within using the same basic steps as the ones shown here; simply choose **New Task for Contact** from the **Action** menu in step 2.

Creating a Mailing List

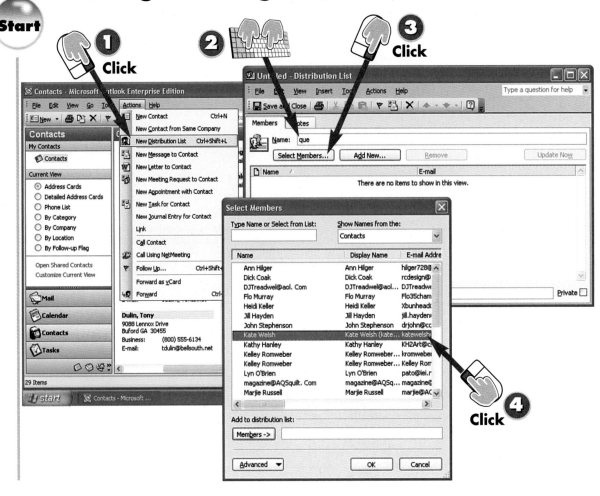

Start

1 **Click**

2

3 **Click**

4 **Click**

① In the main Contacts window, open the **Actions** menu and choose **New Distribution List**.

② A Distribution List window opens. In the **Name** field, type a name to identify the list.

③ Click the **Select Members** button to add group members to the list.

④ The Select Members dialog box opens, featuring a list of your contacts. Click a name to add it to the list.

143

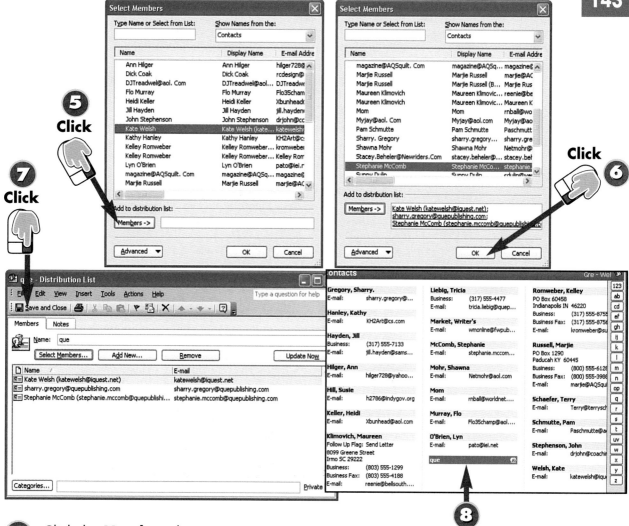

5 Click the **Members** button.

6 Repeat steps 4 and 5 for each contact you want to add to the mailing list. When you finish adding contacts, click the **OK** button.

7 The Distribution List window lists the contacts you added. Click the **Save and Close** button.

8 The group is included in the contact list.

End

Adding Notes About a Group

If you want to include more descriptive information about a group, you can do so in the Distribution List window's Notes tab.

Sending a Message to a Mailing List

Start

Click **2**

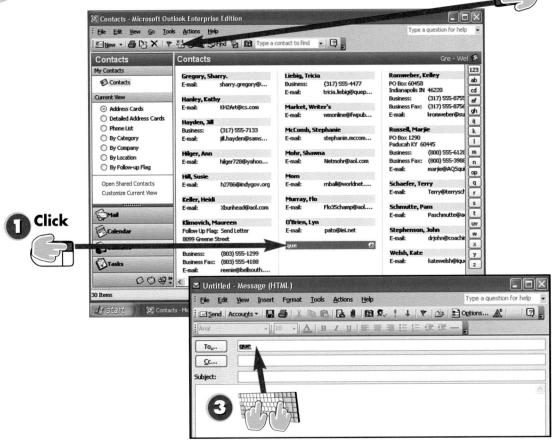

1 Click

3

① In the contact list, click the mailing list to select it.

② Click the **New Message to Contact** button on the main Outlook toolbar.

③ An Untitled Message window opens, featuring the group name in the **To** field. Type a subject for the message in the **Subject** field.

After you have set up a mailing list, creating e-mail messages to send to the group is a snap. You can do so from within the Contacts window (shown here) or from the Mail window.

TIP

Sending from the Mail Window
To send a message to a distribution list from within Outlook's Mail window, create the message and then click the **To** button. Select the mailing list from the contact list that appears, and then click **To**. Complete and send the e-mail message as normal. See Part 2 for more information about sending e-mail.

Click 5

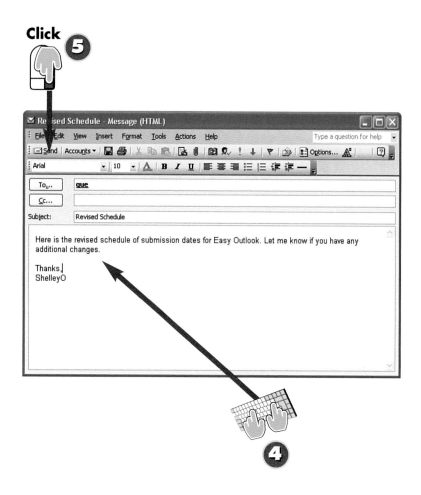

4 Click in the message area and type the contents of the message.

5 Click the **Send** button. Assuming you are online and have set up Outlook to automatically send your messages, the message will be sent.

End

Adding More Names
TIP

Suppose you plan to send a message to a group, but want to include a few additional recipients (without adding those recipients to the group itself). You can add other recipients to the To, Cc, or Bcc fields using the regular process: Display the Select Names dialog box, select a name, and click the appropriate button (**To**, **Cc**, or **Bcc**).

Editing a Mailing List

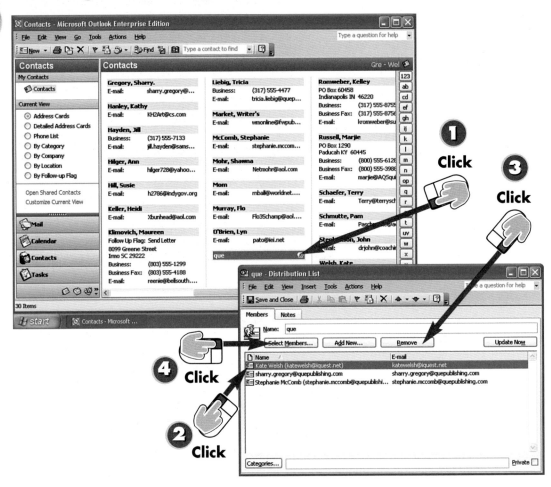

1 In the contact list, double-click the mailing list.

2 The Distribution List window opens, featuring the names of current list members. To remove a member, click his or her name in the list.

3 Click the **Remove** button. The contact is removed from the list.

4 To add a new member, click the **Select Members** button.

Your mailing list may change from time to time. For example, if you've built a mailing list that contains all the people who are working with you on a particular project, and one of the team members leaves the company, you'll want to update the list to reflect the change. Alternatively, you may need to add more people to the list as your team grows. You can easily view and make changes to the contacts included in a mailing list.

No Names Listed?

If no names are listed in the Select Members dialog box, or if the names you need do not appear, it may be because the wrong contact list is being displayed. Click the **down-arrow** next to the **Show Names From The** field and choose the correct contact list from the drop-down list that appears.

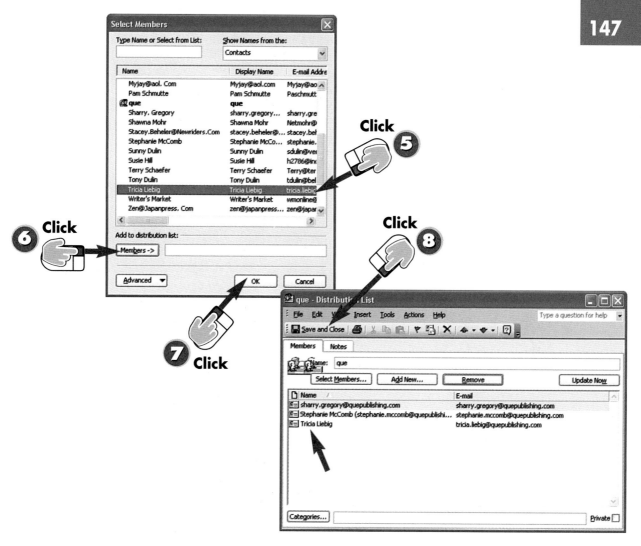

5 The Select Members dialog box opens, featuring a list of your contacts. Click a name to add it to the list.

6 Click the **Members** button.

7 Repeat steps 5 and 6 for each contact you want to add to the mailing list. When you finish adding contacts, click the **OK** button.

8 The new members are added to the list. Click the **Save and Close** button in the Distribution List window to save the changes.

The Add New Button

TIP

Although it seems like you should, you don't use the **Add New** button in the Distribution List window to add names to a mailing list. Instead, you click this button to create an entirely new contact record. Click **Add New** to open an Untitled Contact window, and then add the contact information as usual.

Journaling Activities for a Contact

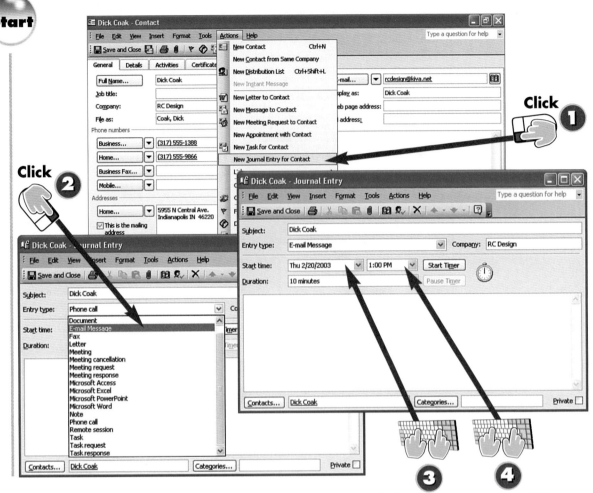

Start

Click 1

Click 2

3

4

1. Open the contact and then open the **Actions** menu and choose **New Journal Entry for Contact**.

2. The Journal Entry window opens with the contact's name in the Subject field. Click the **down-arrow** next to the **Entry Type** field and select the type of entry.

3. Type the date that the activity took place into the **Start Time** field, or click the **down-arrow** next to the field and use the calendar to select the date.

4. Type the activity's start time into the field next to the one containing the start date, or click the **down-arrow** next to the field to choose the start time from the drop-down list.

You may want to jot down notes, summarize discussions, and add other information about a contact. To do so, you can keep a contact journal. Using the contact journal, you can make note of documents sent, requested tasks, e-mail messages, phone calls, and more. These activities are then listed as part of the contact record.

TIP

A Shortcut
If you prefer, simply click—rather than open—the contact for which you want to add a journal entry in the contact list, and then open the **Actions** menu and choose **New Journal Entry for Contact**.

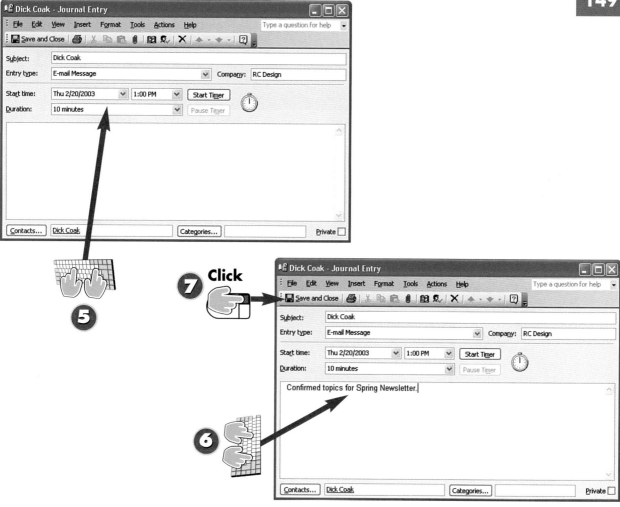

5 In the **Duration** field, type the activity's duration, or click the **down-arrow** to the right of the field to select the duration from a drop-down list.

6 Type a descriptive note for the entry.

7 Click the **Save and Close** button in the Journal Entry window to add the journal entry.

End

Timing a Task

TIP

If you bill by the hour, you might like to enter your journal entry as you perform the task you're recording. When you do, you can then use Outlook's Timer feature to record the time you spend on the task. Click the **Start Timer** button in the Journal Entry window to start the timer; click the **Pause Timer** button when the activity is complete.

Adding Other Journal Entries

TIP

You can add other associated contacts or assign a category to a journal entry. To do so, click the Contacts or Categories button, respectively, in the Journal Entry window.

Viewing a Contact Journal

Start

1 Double-Click

2 Click

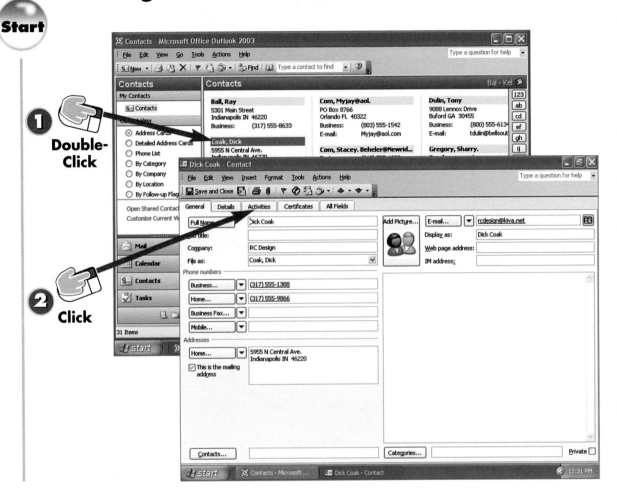

1 In the contact list, double-click the contact whose journal you want to review.

2 In the Contact window, click the **Activities** tab.

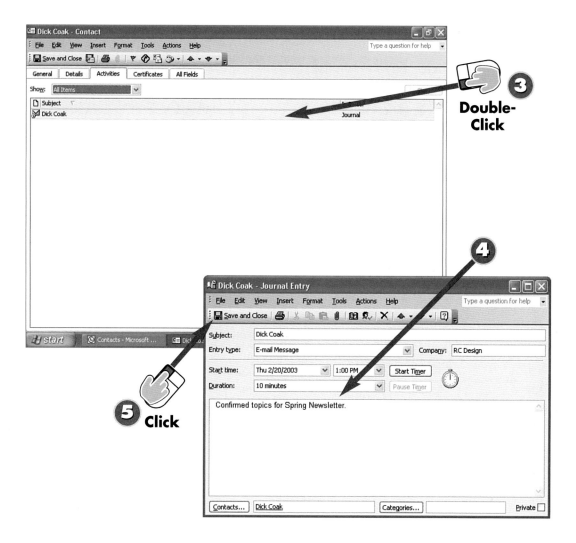

③ A list of all journal entries for this contact appears. To open and view a particular journal entry, double-click it in the list.

④ The Journal Entry window opens, containing the journal entry you selected. Review it and make changes if needed.

⑤ Click the **Save and Close** button in the Journal Entry window to close (and update, if you made changes) the journal entry.

End

Deleting an Entry
To delete a journal entry, click it in the list shown in the Activities tab of the Contact window, and then press the **Delete** key on your keyboard. The item is moved to the Deleted Items folder (for more information about this folder, refer to Part 3 of this book).

Adding Journal Entries Automatically
You can automatically track certain activities for contacts, such as e-mail messages, meeting requests, and tasks. See the next task for more information.

Setting Contact and Journal Options

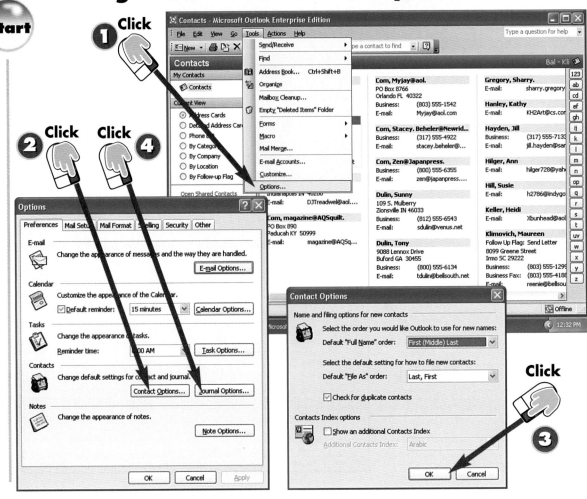

① In the main Contacts window, open the **Tools** menu and choose **Options**.

② The Options dialog box opens. To view or change contact options, click the **Contact Options** button.

③ Change how the contact is displayed and filed and whether a Contacts index is displayed. When you're finished, click **OK**.

④ Click the **Journal Options** button.

INTRODUCTION

If the default settings for contacts or journal entries do not suit how you work, you can change them. For example, for contacts, you can change the format in which the contact name is displayed. For journal options, you can select which activities are automatically recorded.

TIP

Setting Contact Options
For Contact options, you can basically select the order they appear and how they are filed. The default order is First, (Middle), Last and the default file order is Last, First.

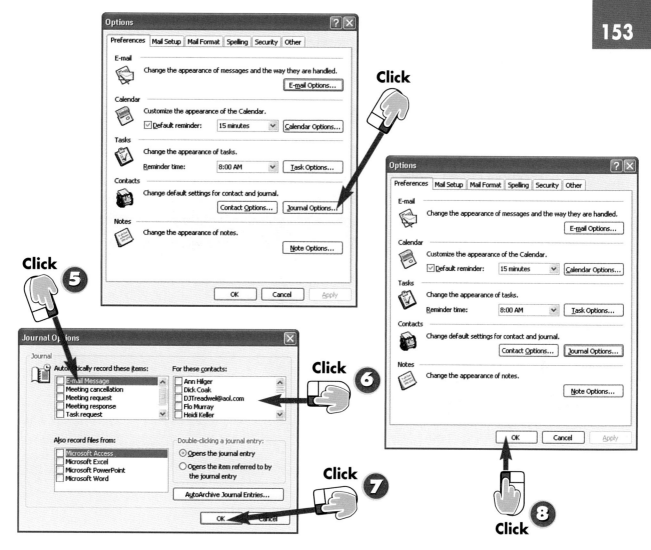

The Journal Options dialog box opens. Click to select the check boxes next to any activities or files that you want automatically recorded in your journal.

Click to select the check boxes next to the contacts for which you want to record the items selected in step 5.

Click **OK** to close the Journal Options dialog box.

Click **OK** to update both the contact and journal options and to close the Options dialog box.

Viewing Journal Activities
You can view any automatically journaled activities for a contact. See "Viewing a Contact Journal" for more information.

AutoArchive Journal Entries
Journal entries are archived using the default AutoArchive settings. If you want to use other settings (archive at a different interval, use a different archive folder, for instance), click **AutoArchive Journal Entries**, make your selections, and click **OK**.

Keeping a Calendar

In addition to the Mail and Contact features, Outlook includes a scheduling program called, aptly, Calendar. You can use this feature to keep track of meetings, appointments, and other events. Outlook will conveniently remind you beforehand of upcoming events. Also, you can print a calendar in one of several handy formats. This section covers the various ways you can use Calendar to manage your time.

The Calendar Window

menu bar ▶

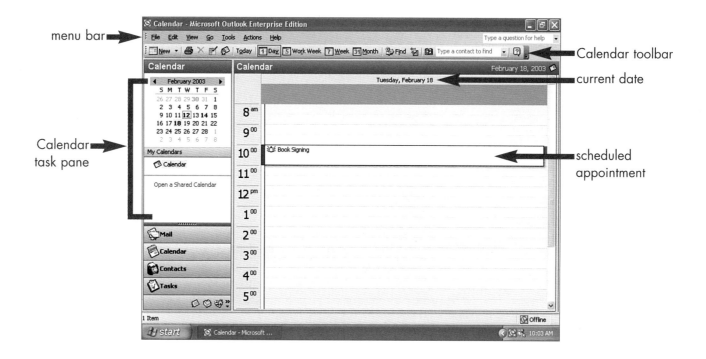

Calendar toolbar

current date

Calendar
task pane ▶

scheduled
appointment

Viewing the Calendar Window

Start

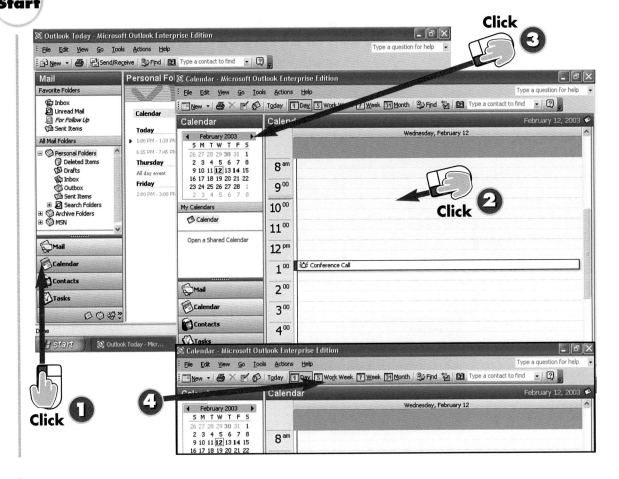

1 After starting Outlook, click **Calendar** in the Outlook Bar.

2 Calendar opens, displaying today's calendar. The main window breaks up the day into hours and displays any scheduled events.

3 The task pane displays the current month. Click any date in that month to view its scheduled activities.

4 The toolbar includes buttons for scheduling and managing events as well as for changing the view.

End

Accessing Calendar
You can also change to Calendar (and other Outlook features) by opening the **Go** menu and choosing **Calendar**. Alternatively, press the Calendar shortcut key, **Ctrl+2**.

Handling Early-Morning Events
When you display a date, Outlook displays 8 a.m. as the top line in the main work area. You can schedule and view events earlier than 8 a.m. by clicking the scroll buttons along the right side of the Outlook window.

Changing Calendar Views

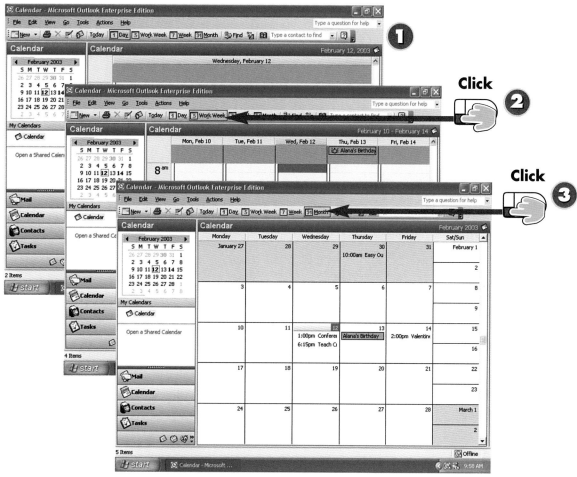

1 The default view is Day view, showing a single day.

2 To view the work week (Monday through Friday), click the **Work Week** toolbar button. The main window changes to show Calendar entries for the entire work week.

3 To view the entire month, click the **Month** toolbar button. The main window changes to show Calendar entries for the entire month.

INTRODUCTION

To help you manage your schedule, you can change to other Calendar views. For example, suppose you want to see an overview of the week's events. In that case, you can choose to view either the work week (Monday through Friday) or the "regular" week (Monday through Sunday).

TIP

Using the View Menu
You can also use the View menu to change to a different calendar view. Click **View** and then select **Day**, **Work Week**, **Week**, or **Month**.

TIP

Changing Calendar Options
To view the seven-day week (Monday through Sunday), click the **Week** toolbar button. The main window changes to show Calendar entries for the entire seven-day week.

Viewing a Particular Date

Start

Click ②

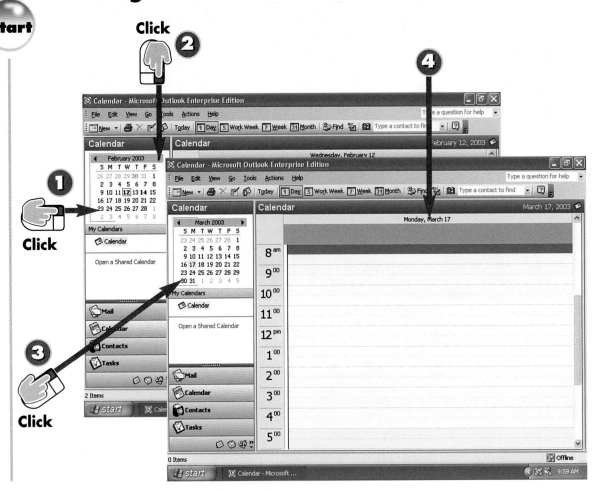

① Click

③ Click

④

① If the date you want to view is in the current month, simply click it in the minicalendar located in the task pane.

② If the date you want to view is in another month, click the scroll arrows in the minicalendar until the correct month appears.

③ When the month you want is displayed in the task pane, click the date you want to view.

④ The calendar for that date is displayed.

TIP

Returning to Today
To return to the current day's calendar, click the **Today** toolbar button. Alternatively, click the current date in the minicalendar on the task pane (it's the date boxed in red).

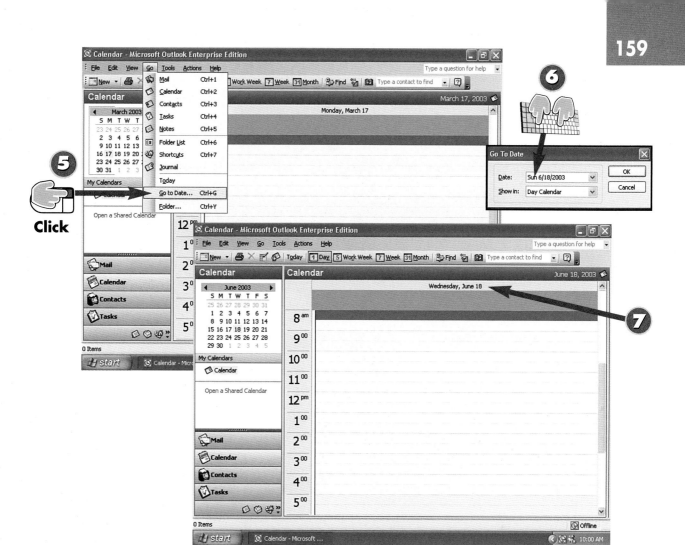

Click

5️⃣ If the date you want to view is several months away, scrolling through the minicalendar can be time consuming. In that case, click the **Go** menu, and then click **Go to Date**.

6️⃣ The Go to Date dialog box opens. Type the date you want to see and click **OK**.

7️⃣ The date you typed is displayed.

End

Using Shortcut Keys
TIP If you prefer to use your keyboard instead of menus, press **Ctrl+G** to open the Go to Date dialog box.

Scheduling an Appointment

Start

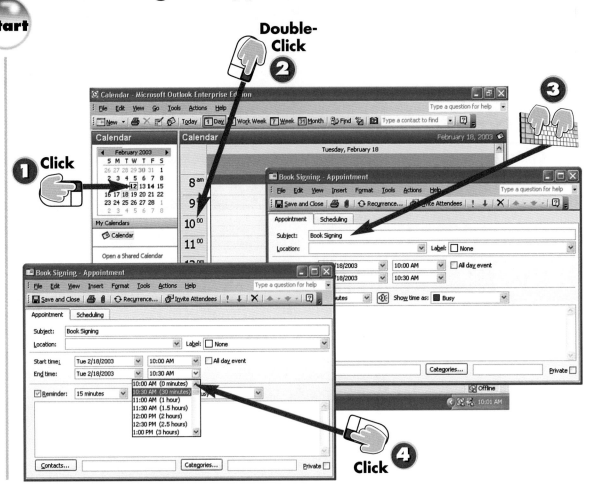

Double-Click 2

3

Click 1

Click 4

---

1 Display the date on which the event you want to schedule is planned. (For help displaying dates, see the preceding task.)

2 Double-click the start time of the event. The Untitled Appointment window opens with the start time and end time filled in.

3 In the **Subject** field, type a name for the appointment (in this example, **Book Signing**). This text will appear on the calendar and in the title bar of the Appointment window.

4 By default, appointments last for 30 minutes. To change the end time, click the **down-arrow** button to the right of the **End Time** field and select a time.

INTRODUCTION

Your calendar is useful only if you take the time to enter your appointments, meetings, and events into it. Then you can quickly view what's planned for a particular date.

TIP

Using the New Button
While you're in Calendar view, you can also click the **New** button on the toolbar to open the Untitled Appointment window.

TIP

Changing the Date and Start Time
If you need to change the start date or start time, do so using the **Start Time** drop-down list boxes in the Appointment window.

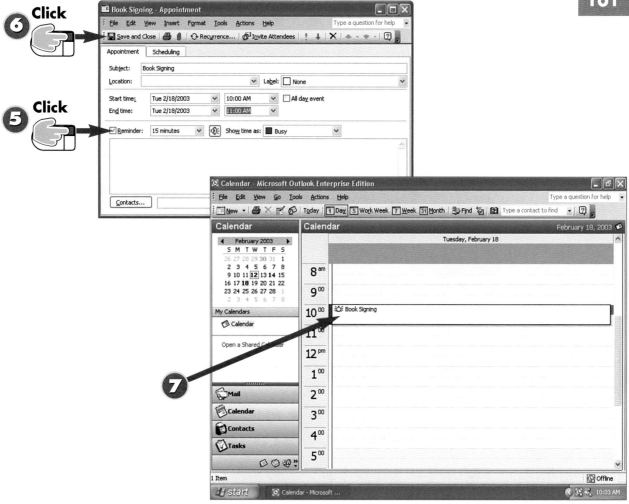

Click 6

Click 5

5 By default, Outlook displays a reminder alert box 15 minutes before the appointment is to begin. To turn off the reminder, uncheck the **Reminder** check box.

6 Click the **Save and Close** button.

7 The appointment is added to your calendar.

End

Location and Description
You can type a location into the **Location** field (this information appears in parentheses after the appointment subject in the calendar) and a description into the **Notes** area at the bottom of the window.

Scheduling All-Day Events
To schedule an all-day event, check the **All Day Event** check box. All-day events are not blocked out on the day calendar, but are listed at the top of that day.

Opening and Editing Existing Appointments

Start

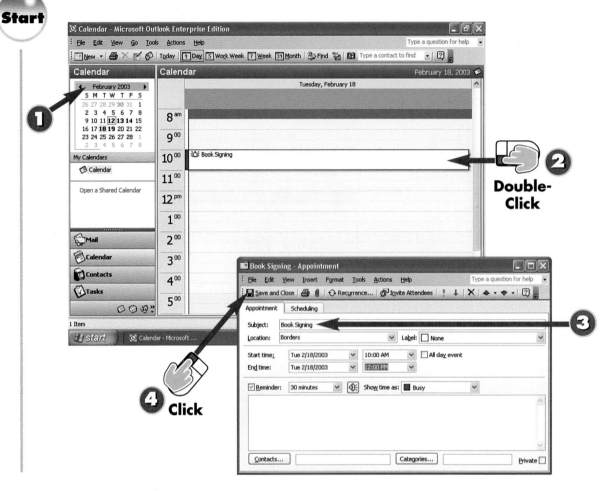

Double-Click

Click

1. Display the date that contains the appointment you want to open. (For more information, refer to "Viewing a Particular Date" earlier in this part.)

2. Double-click the appointment you want to open.

3. The selected event's Appointment window opens, displaying the details of the scheduled event. Make changes to the appointment information as needed.

4. Click the **Save and Close** button to update the event.

End

INTRODUCTION

No doubt there will be times when you'll want to view the details of a scheduled appointment, either to verify a time or to change some aspect of the event.

TIP

Handling Scheduling Conflicts
If you schedule two appointments that overlap, the Appointment window displays the message **Conflicts with Another Appointment on Your Calendar**. You are not notified of this problem when you save and close the appointment, so be sure to keep a careful eye on double-booked times.

Labeling and Marking Appointments

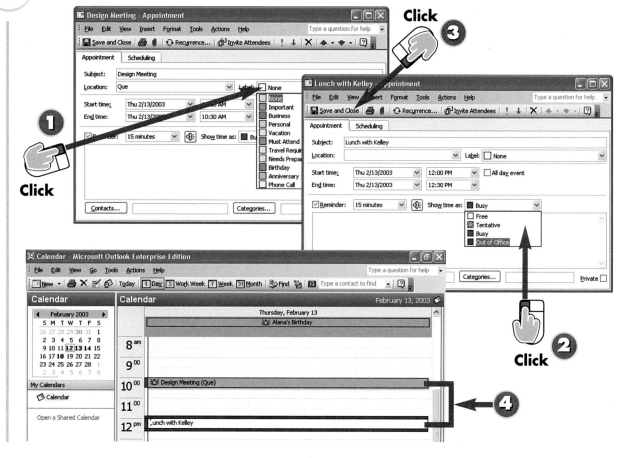

① With the appointment displayed, click the **down-arrow** button next to the **Label** field and select a label from the list that appears.

② To change how the time for the appointment appears, click the **down-arrow** next to the **Show Time As** field and select an option.

③ Click the **Save and Close** button in the **Appointment** window.

④ Color-coded labeled events help you see at a glance the event type; time-coded events are indicated with a border.

INTRODUCTION

You have several options for coding your scheduled appointments. First, you can label an event. You have several options ranging from importance to personal to event type (birthday, for example). Second, you can select how the time is displayed in your calendar; you can choose Free, Tentative, Busy, or Out of Office.

Editing Label
To change the label for an event, select the event, open the **Edit** menu and choose **Label**, and select the label you want to apply.

Using Other Options
You can also mark an appointment as high or low importance using the **Importance: High** or **Importance: Low** buttons in the Appointment window. To mark an appointment as private, check the **Private** check box.

Assigning a Category to an Appointment

Start

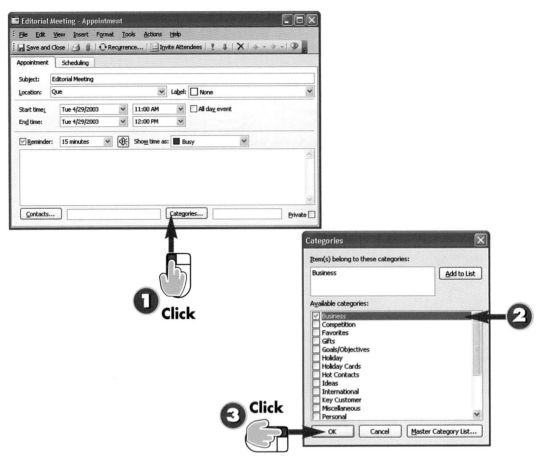

Click

Click

1 With the appointment displayed, click the **Categories** button in the Appointment window.

2 The Categories dialog box opens, displaying a list of available categories. Mark the check box next to any categories you want to assign to the appointment.

3 Click **OK**.

INTRODUCTION

To organize your appointments, you can assign each one a category (such as personal or business) . You can then view all appointments by category. Doing so can help you distinguish the various types of items in your schedule.

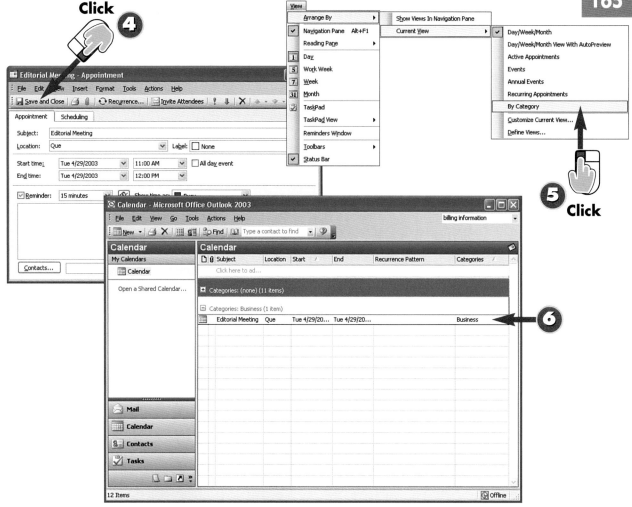

Click

4 The category is listed with the appointment details. Click the **Save and Close** button.

5 To view your appointments by category, open the **View** menu, choose **Arrange By**, select **Current View**, and then click **By Category**.

6 Outlook displays a list of your appointments, arranged by category.

End

Expanding and Collapsing the List
You can display more (or less) information for the selected appointments for each category. Click the plus sign (+) next to a category to expand the item and display all appointments. Click the minus sign (−) to hide the appointments.

No Category?
If you have not assigned categories to other appointments, they are all grouped together in the Category view.

PART 6

Listing Contacts for an Appointment

Start

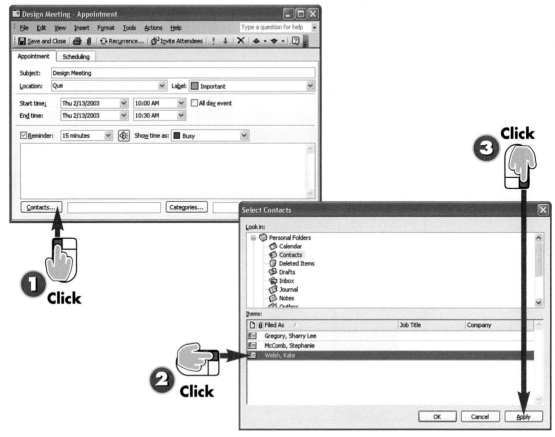

Click

3

1 Click

2 Click

1 After you've scheduled a new appointment or opened an existing one, click the **Contacts** button in the Appointment window.

2 The Select Contacts dialog box opens. Click the first contact you want to add to the appointment.

3 Click the **Apply** button.

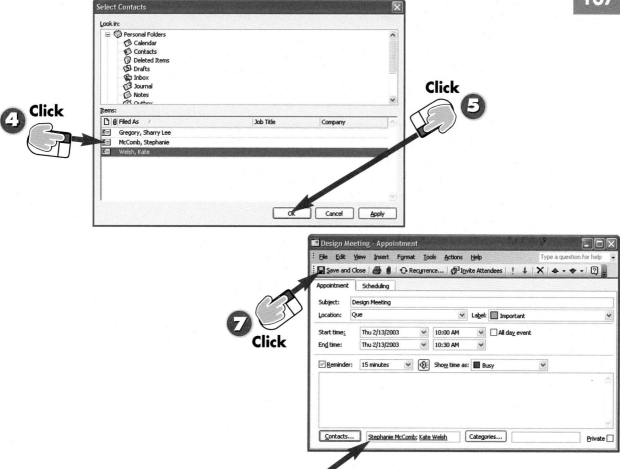

4 Repeat steps 2 and 3 for each additional contact you want to add.

5 When you're finished adding contacts to the appointment, click **OK**.

6 The contacts are listed in the Appointment window.

7 Click **Save and Close**.

Scheduling a Recurring Appointment

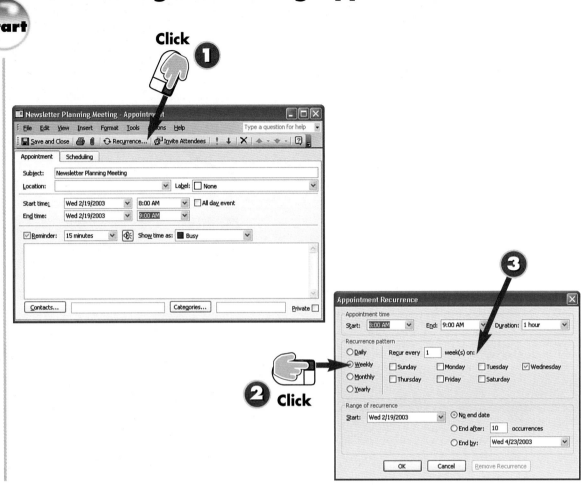

Click ①

② Click

③

1. After you've created a new appointment or opened an existing one, click the **Recurrence** button in the Appointment window.

2. Click the **Daily**, **Weekly**, **Monthly**, or **Yearly** option button to set the recurrence pattern (in this case, **Weekly** is selected).

3. The options for the recurrence pattern vary depending on your selection in step 2. Make your selections.

TIP

Removing a Recurring Appointment
To delete a recurring appointment, select any of the listed appointments in the Calendar and then click the **Delete** button (the one with an X on it) in the Appointment window's toolbar. Outlook asks whether you want to delete only the selected occurrence or the series (all occurrences). Make your choice and click **OK**.

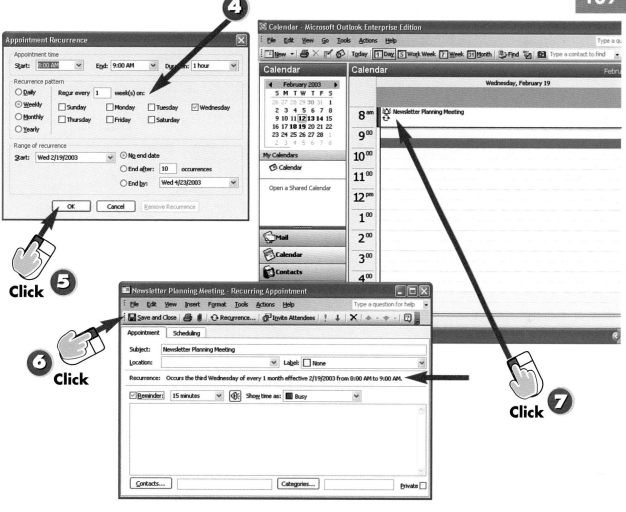

4 Specify the range of recurrence—that is, over what period of time the recurring appointment will occur.

5 Click **OK**.

6 The Appointment window's date and time information lists the recurrence details you entered; click **Save and Close**.

7 The Calendar displays a special icon for recurring appointments.

End

Scheduling a New Appointment
To schedule a new recurring appointment, open the **Actions** menu and select **New Recurring Appointment**.

Editing a Recurring Appointment
Double-click the appointment. When prompted, select whether to edit just that specific instance (**Open This Occurrence**) or every future appointment (**Open the Series**). Then make changes as needed

Setting Reminders

Start

Double-Click ❶

Click ❷

❸ **Click**

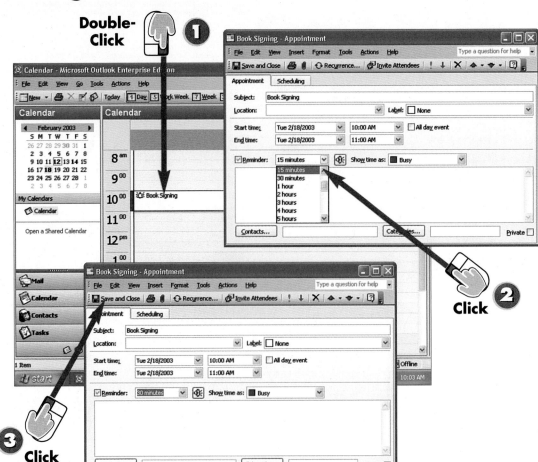

❶ To set a reminder for an appointment, first double-click the appointment in Calendar to open its Appointment window.

❷ To change the lead time for the reminder, click the **down-arrow** button to the right of the **Reminder** field and select the desired lead time from the list that appears.

❸ Click the **Save and Close** button.

End

Handling Reminders

Start

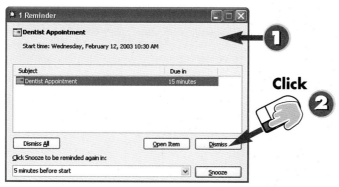

Click ②

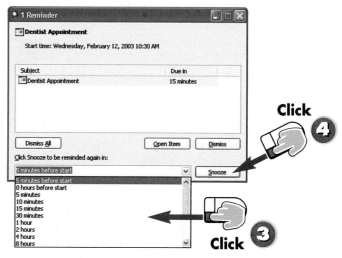

Click ④

Click ③

① When a Reminder dialog box appears, you'll see the appointment name, its start time, and the date.

② To dismiss the reminder (and turn off the alert), click the **Dismiss** button; the Reminder dialog box closes.

③ If you want to receive a second reminder, select a **Snooze** interval from the drop-down list at the bottom of the Reminder dialog box.

④ Click the **Snooze** button.

End

Scheduling a Meeting

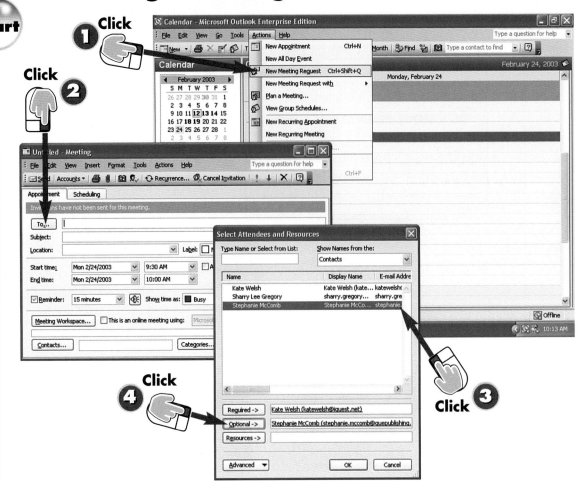

Start

Click ① **Click** ② **Click** ③ **Click** ④

---

① Open the **Actions** menu and choose **New Meeting Request**.

② The Untitled Meeting window opens; it includes many of the same options as an Appointment window. Click the **To** button to add contacts.

③ The Select Attendees and Resources dialog box opens. From the list of contacts, select a person you want to invite to the meeting.

④ Click the **Required** button or **Optional** button, depending on the selected contact's attendance. The selected contact is added to the list of invitees.

INTRODUCTION

Outlook handles meetings a little differently from run-of-the-mill appointments. To schedule a meeting, you specify the contacts who are invited to attend, enter in meeting details, and email the group to set up the meeting.

TIP

Getting Help with Email
For detailed information on sending email messages, see Part 2 of this book. (For more information on contacts, see Part V of this book.)

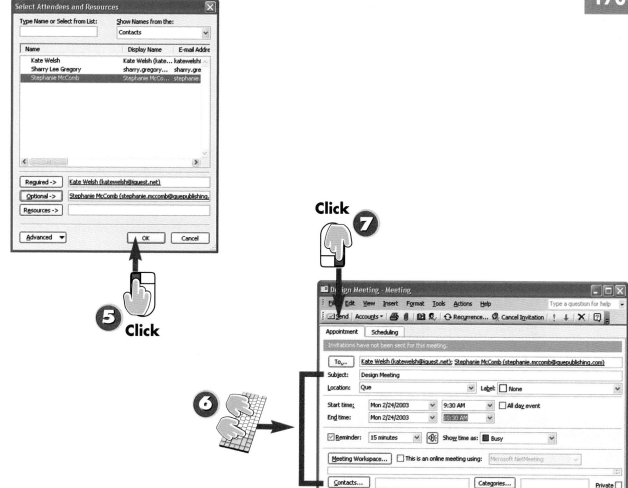

5 Repeat steps 3 and 4 for each person you want to invite. When you're finished adding contacts, click **OK**.

6 Complete the meeting details as you would for a regular appointment—by setting a subject, a location, start and end dates and times, and a reminder.

7 Click **Send**. The meeting request is emailed to the invitees. When you receive the responses, you can confirm the meeting time.

Handling Meeting Requests

When an invitee receives a meeting request, he or she can accept, decline, propose a new time, or give a tentative answer. When you receive that invitee's reply, you can confirm the meeting.

Scheduling Resources

You can use Outlook to schedule *resources*, such as conference or training rooms. In that case, Outlook sends a message to the person who schedules those rooms, who can verify the resource's availability and then accept or decline on behalf of the resource.

Searching for an Appointment

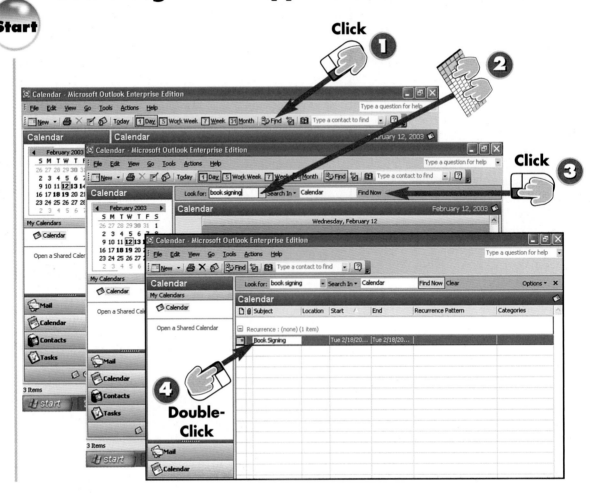

Start

Click ①

②

Click ③

Double-Click ④

---

① In Calendar, click the **Find** button on the Outlook toolbar.

② A special Find bar appears. In the **Look For** field, type a word or phrase that identifies the appointment you seek.

③ Click the **Find Now** button.

④ Outlook displays matching items. To open a matched item, double-click it. To close the search results, click the **Close** button on the far right side of the Find bar.

End

INTRODUCTION

You can easily scroll through dates to view upcoming appointments. If you are looking for a particular event and are not sure when it is scheduled, however, use the **Find** button.

TIP

Setting Search Options
You can change the search options by clicking the **Options** button and then clicking **Advanced Find**. Use it to search by many other criteria, such as attendees, scheduled time, or importance.

TIP

Searching Other Outlook Areas
You can use the **Search In** drop-down list to select to search other Outlook areas, including various mail folders, tasks, and so on.

Deleting an Appointment

Start

Click 3

Click 1

Click 2

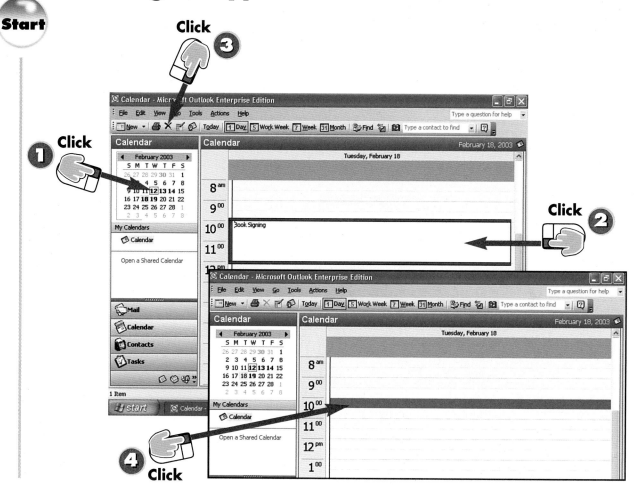

4 **Click**

1. Using the minicalendar in the task pane, display the date that contains the appointment you want to open.

2. Click the appointment you want to delete.

3. Click the **Delete** button on the Outlook toolbar.

4. The item is removed from the Calendar.

End

If you find that you need to cancel a scheduled appointment, you can delete it from your calendar. Doing so will help you keep track of which appointments were kept and which were not.

TIP

Deleting a Meeting
To delete a meeting from the Calendar, perform steps 1–3 in this task. Outlook asks whether you want to email a cancellation notice to other meeting participants; choose **Send Cancellation and Delete meeting** or **Delete Without Sending a Cancellation**. Then click **OK**.

Setting Up a Calendar for Printing

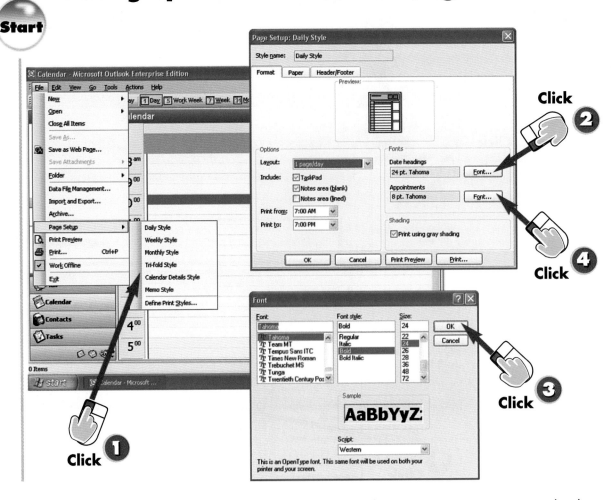

① Open the **File** menu and choose **Page Setup**. A submenu containing various calendar styles appears; choose the style you want to use for your printout.

② To change the font for the date headings, click the **Font** button to the right of the **Date Headings** field.

③ The Font dialog box opens. Choose a font, style, and size for the date headings, and click **OK**.

④ Back in the Page Setup dialog box, change the font for the appointments by clicking the **Font** button to the right of the **Appointments** field; repeat step 3 to assign the desired fonts.

TIP

Understanding the Options
The Page Setup options vary depending on the selected printout style. If you are unsure about an option, right-click it and select **What's This?** to view a brief description.

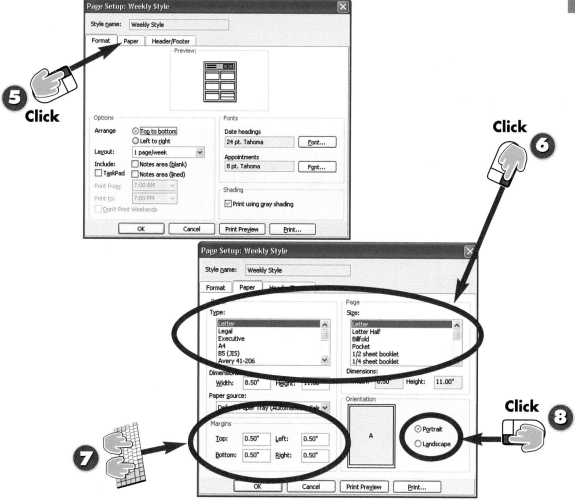

5 To print a calendar on special paper or change the orientation to better suit the data, click the **Paper** tab in the Page Setup dialog box.

6 Using the **Type** and **Size** lists, select from any number of available paper types and sizes.

7 To change the margins, type new values in the **Top**, **Bottom**, **Left**, or **Right** fields.

8 To change the page's orientation, click the **Landscape** or **Portrait** option button. When you're finished, click **OK**.

End

Previewing and Printing
You can preview or print the Calendar directly from the Page Setup dialog box by clicking the **Print Preview** or **Print** button.

Including Headers and Footers
You can add a header or a footer to the printout using the Page Setup dialog box's Header/Footer tab. Specify where the text should appear (at the left margin, centered, or at the right margin) and type the text to include. You can also, if you want, use the handy buttons to insert common header and footer items such as page numbers or dates.

Previewing a Calendar Printout

Start

Click ②

Click ①

Click ④

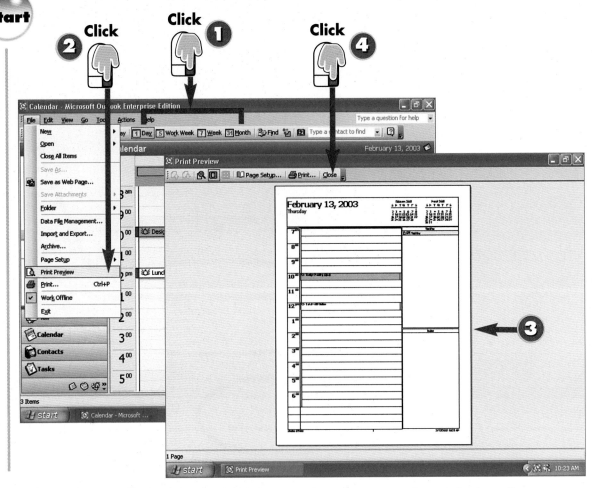

1. Click the **Day**, **Work Week**, **Week**, or **Month** button on the Outlook toolbar to choose the desired Calendar view.

2. Open the **File** menu and choose **Print Preview**.

3. A preview of the Calendar printout appears. (Outlook uses different print styles for each of these views.)

4. When you are finished previewing the printout, click the **Close** (x) button.

End

INTRODUCTION

Before you print a calendar, you may want to preview the printout. Previewing is also a handy way to get an idea of the default setup for each of the calendar styles.

Changing the Setup
TIP
If you don't care for the appearance of the printout, you can change it using the Page Setup dialog box. For more information about using this dialog box, see the preceding task.

Printing from the Print Preview Window
TIP
You can print directly from Print Preview by clicking the **Print** button at the top of the window.

Printing a Calendar

Start

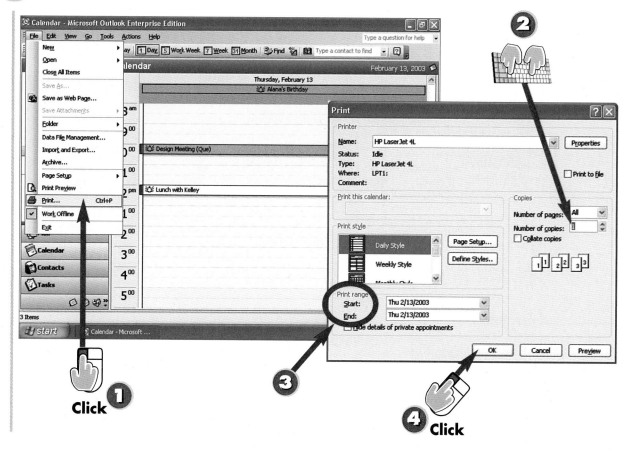

Click ①

③

Click ④

① After you've selected **Day**, **Work Week**, **Week**, or **Month** view, open the **File** menu and choose **Print**.

② In the **Number of Copies** field, type the number of copies you want to print.

③ Using the **Start** and **End** drop-down lists in the **Print Range** area, specify the days you want your printout to include.

④ Click **OK** to print your calendar.

End

INTRODUCTION

If you need a hard copy of your schedule, you can print your calendar. To print your daily or weekly schedule, start in **Day**, **Work Week**, or **Week** view. To print a month-at-a-glance, start in **Month** view.

TIP

Changing the Print Style
Outlook automatically selects the print style that matches the current Calendar view. If needed, however, you can change to another style by selecting it from the **Print Style** list in the Print dialog box.

TIP

Using Print Shortcuts
If you prefer using Outlook's toolbars to its menus, click the **Print** button to open the Print dialog box. Alternatively, press **Ctrl+P**.

Setting Calendar Options

Start

Click 1

Click 3

Click 2

Click 4

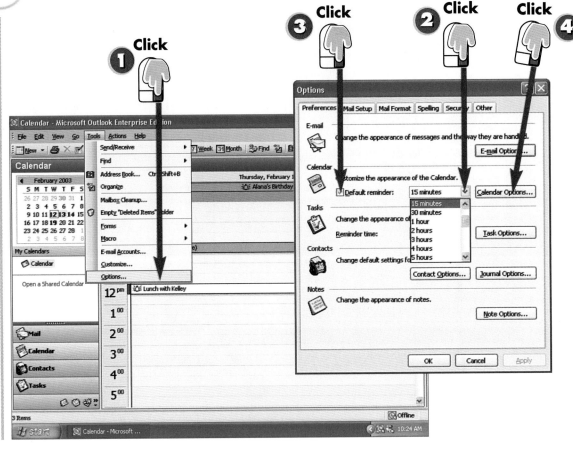

1 Open the **Tools** menu and choose **Options**.

2 To change the default reminder lead time, click the **down-arrow** button next to the **Default Reminder** field and choose a new lead time.

3 To disable Outlook's default reminder option altogether, uncheck the **Default Reminder** check box.

4 To make other changes, click the **Calendar Options** button.

Most of the default settings for Calendar work fairly well. If, however, you have a unique schedule (for example, if you have an unusual work week) or want to change other settings such as those related to reminders, you can do so using Calendar's Options dialog box.

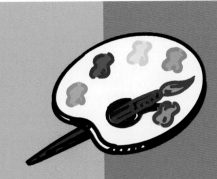

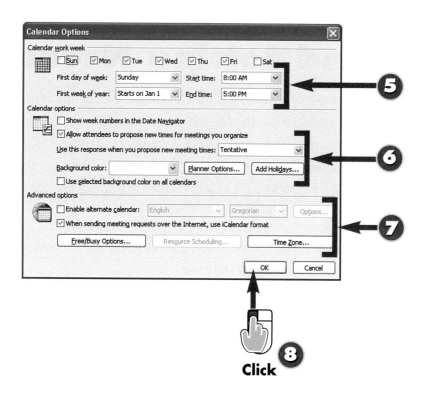

Click

⑤ To change the Calendar work week, add a check mark to each day that should be included and specify the first day of the week and year.

⑥ Change settings as needed, such as those related to how meeting requests are handled, in the **Calendar Options** area.

⑦ In the **Advanced Options** area, change settings, such as the time zone, as desired.

⑧ Click **OK** in the Calendar Options dialog box and again in the Options dialog box to close it.

End

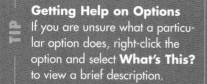

Getting Help on Options
If you are unsure what a particular option does, right-click the option and select **What's This?** to view a brief description.

Using Group Scheduling
Outlook includes tools for managing group schedules and online meeting planning. For information on these advanced features, consult Outlook's Help system.

Creating a To-Do List and Jotting Notes

Yet another component of Outlook is the Tasks list. Using this feature, you can add tasks that you need to complete and then view, manage, and keep track of your upcoming, completed, and overdue tasks. Using the Tasks list will help you note relevant dates; for example, you may track when you submitted proposals or when you completed a project. Using the Tasks list can also help you keep track of time and expenses.

This part covers using Tasks for managing your to-do list as well as Notes. You can use Notes to jot reminders to yourself.

The Tasks Window

Menu bar

Toolbar

Task pane

Task list

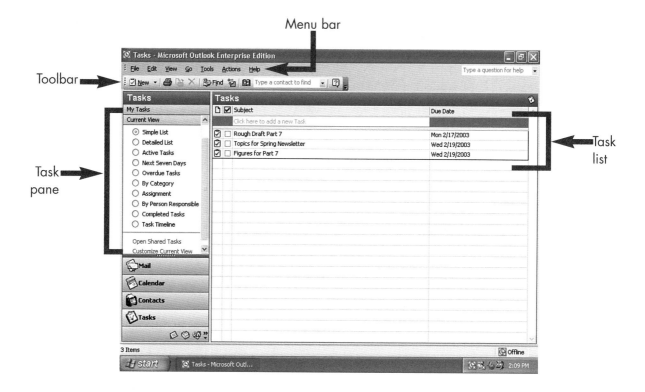

Viewing the Tasks Window

Start

Click ①

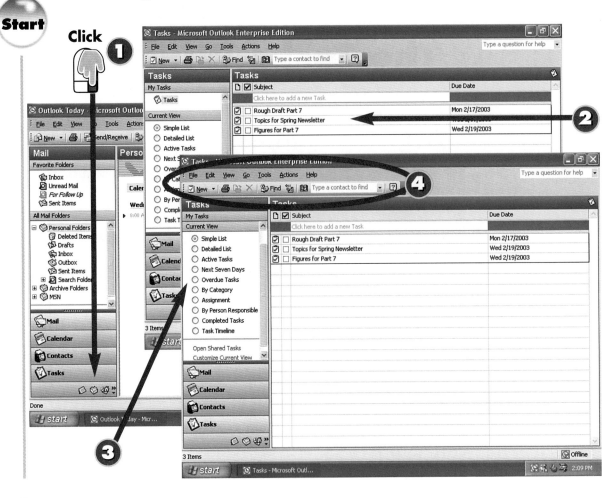

① After starting Outlook, click **Tasks** in the Outlook Bar.

② Scheduled tasks are listed in the main area of the Tasks window.

③ The task pane enables you to select different views of your Tasks list. (You learn more about using categories, marking tasks as complete, and other options later in this part.)

④ The toolbar includes buttons for creating and managing tasks.

End

As with other Outlook components, you can switch to the Tasks window and then view any scheduled tasks. You can also get an idea of what you can do with Tasks by viewing the task pane and toolbar.

Switching to the Tasks Window
You can also switch to the Tasks window by opening the **Go** menu and choosing **Tasks**. Alternatively, press **Ctrl+4**.

Changing the View of the Tasks List

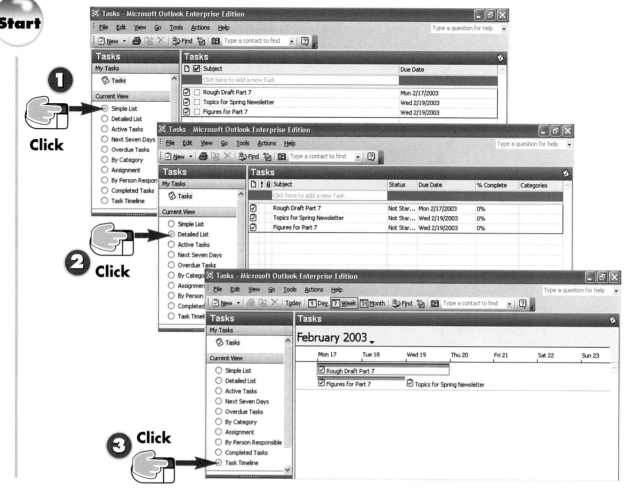

The current view is indicated in the task pane by a selected option button (in this case, **Simple List**, the default view).

Click the **Detailed List** option button in the task pane to change to this view. In Detailed List view, you see columns for subject, status, due date, percent complete, and any assigned category.

To view a graphical timeline of scheduled tasks, click **Task Timeline**.

To help you manage your Tasks list, you can change how it is displayed, or its *view*. Outlook provides several predesigned views. Some options, such as Detailed List, change what appears in the list. Some filter the list to include only a range of entries.

Checking the Header Bar
You can tell when Outlook is displaying only a subset of tasks by looking at the Header bar. You'll see **(Filter Applied)** when only some of the tasks are displayed.

Entering a New Task

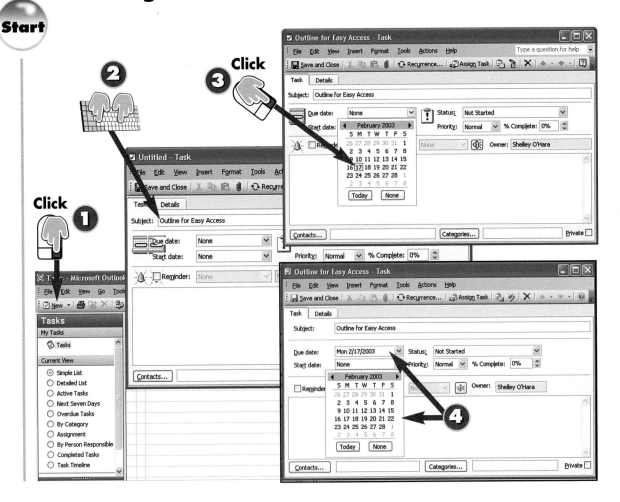

1 With the Tasks window open, click the **New** button on the Outlook toolbar.

2 An Untitled Task dialog box opens. Type a descriptive subject in the Subject field; what you type here is the heading that is used for the task in the Tasks list.

3 Type a due date for the task in the **Due Date** field or click the **down-arrow** button next to the field and choose a date from the minicalendar that appears.

4 If desired, enter a start date for the task by typing a date into the Due Date field or by selecting a date from the minicalendar.

INTRODUCTION

To use Outlook to keep track of tasks, you must first enter information about each task you need to perform. When creating a new task, you can enter a task name, a start date, a due date, the priority, and other details.

Other Ways to Create New Tasks

If you prefer, you can type a task directly into the Tasks list in the area that says **Click Here to Add a New Task**. You can also create a new task by opening the **Actions** menu and choosing **New Task**.

Priority and the Percent Age

You can use the Priority drop-down list to select a priority for the task (**Low**, **Normal**, or **High**). You also can enter information about the progress using the **% Complete** spin box.

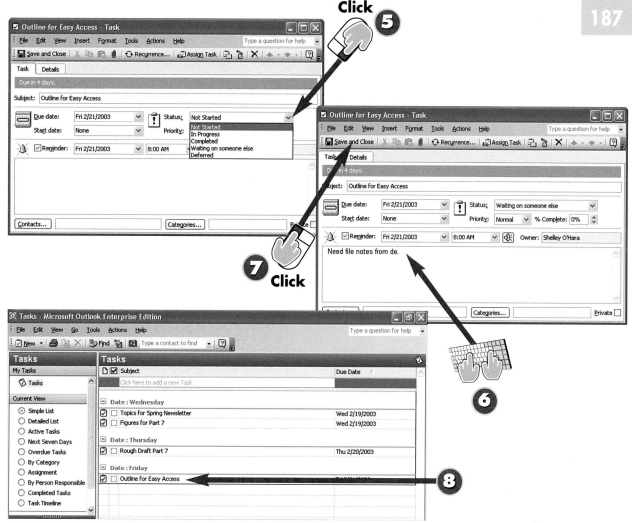

Click

Click

⑤ Click the **down-arrow** button to the right of the **Status** field to display the status options, and select the option that describes the task's current status.

⑥ Type any descriptive information about the task into the Notes area.

⑦ Click the **Save and Close** button in the Tasks window.

⑧ The task is added to the Tasks list.

End

Sorting the List
You can click any of the column headings to sort the Tasks list by that item. For example, click **Subject** to sort in alphabetical order based on the tasks' subjects.

Expanding and Collapsing the List
Outlook groups tasks scheduled within the same timeframe in some views. You can display more (or less) information for the selected tasks in that category. Click the plus sign (+) next to an item to expand the item and display more information. Click the minus sign (−) to hide the details.

Opening and Editing an Existing Task

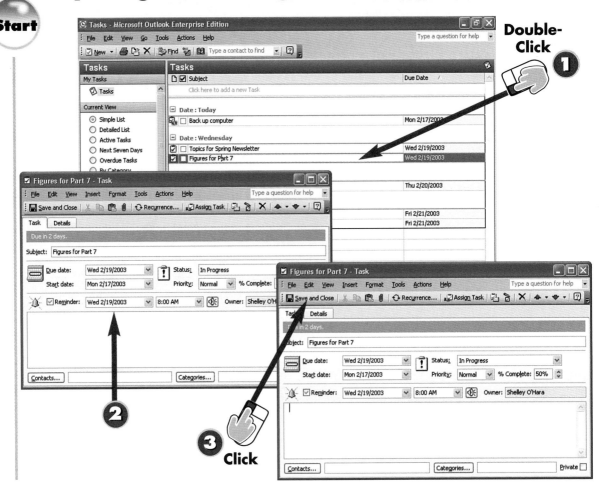

1. Double-click the task you want to open. (You may need to change views first; refer to the task "Changing the View of the Tasks List" earlier in this part for help.)

2. The Tasks window opens, displaying details about the selected task. Make changes to the task as needed.

3. When you are finished editing the task, click the **Save and Close** button. The task information is updated.

End

Start

Double-Click 1

Click 3

2

No doubt there will be times when you'll want to view the details of a task, perhaps to verify or change some aspect of the task.

Selecting a Group of Tasks
Outlook groups task by date (today, tomorrow, and so on). You can easily select several items by clicking the category. For example, to select all tasks scheduled for today, click the heading **Date: Today**.

Editing from the Tasks List
You can also make changes from the Tasks list. Click in any of the displayed fields and make a change. For example, to change the subject, click within this field and then edit the text. Click outside the task to update the item.

Assigning a Task

Start

Click 1

Click 2

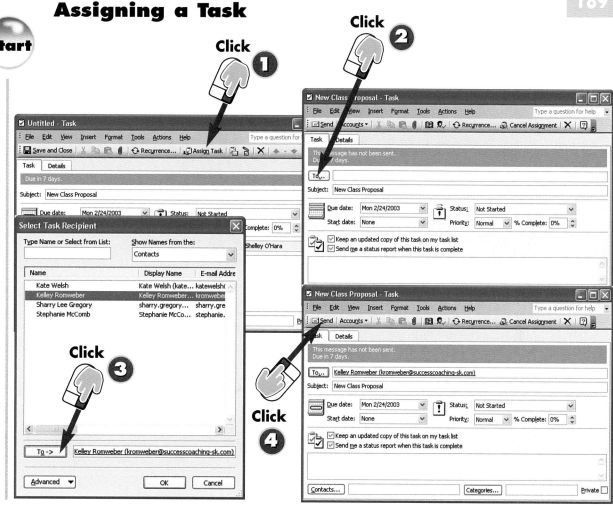

Click 3

Click 4

1. After you've created a new task or opened an existing one, click the **Assign Task** button in the Tasks window.

2. The Tasks window changes to a Message window that includes details about the task. Click the **To** button in the window.

3. Select the person who is assigned to this task from the list and click **To**. The person is added to the message address; click **OK**.

4. Click **Send** to send the message and create the task. Outlook keeps a copy in your Tasks list and will send you a status report when the task is completed.

End

INTRODUCTION

You can use Outlook not only to create a Tasks list, but also to assign a task to an individual. When you assign a task, you enter the task details and send the item as an e-mail message to the appointed person.

TIP

Keeping Contact Information

In addition to assigning tasks, you can also associate contacts with a task. You might do this when others aren't responsible for completing a task, but need to be kept apprised of its status. To do so, click the **Contacts** button in the Tasks window and then select the associated contacts. These names are then added to the task information.

Setting Up Recurring Tasks

Start

Click **1**

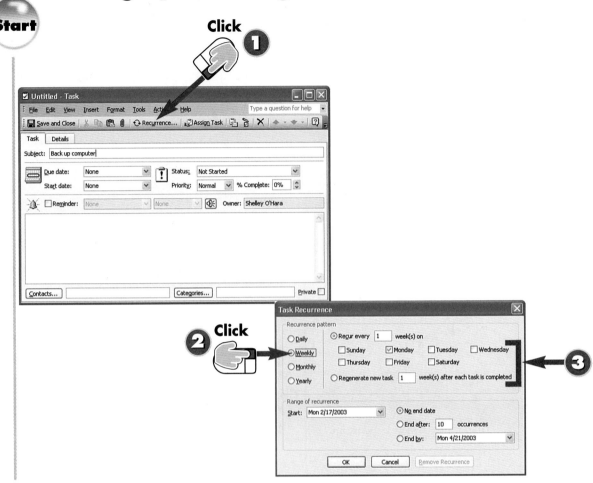

2 **Click**

3

1 After you've created a new task or opened an existing one, click the **Recurrence** button.

2 Click the **Daily**, **Weekly**, **Monthly**, or **Yearly** option button to set the recurrence pattern.

3 The options for the recurrence pattern vary depending on your selection in step 2. Make your selections accordingly.

If you routinely perform a certain task, such as backing up your computer once a week, you can set it up once as a recurring task rather than creating the same task over and over again for each occurrence. You can start by creating a new task or by setting the recurrence for an existing task.

Creating a New Task
To schedule a new recurring task, open the **Actions** menu and select **New Recurring Task**. The Task Recurrence dialog box opens; fill it out as described in this task. Then, in the Tasks window, add the details for the actual task.

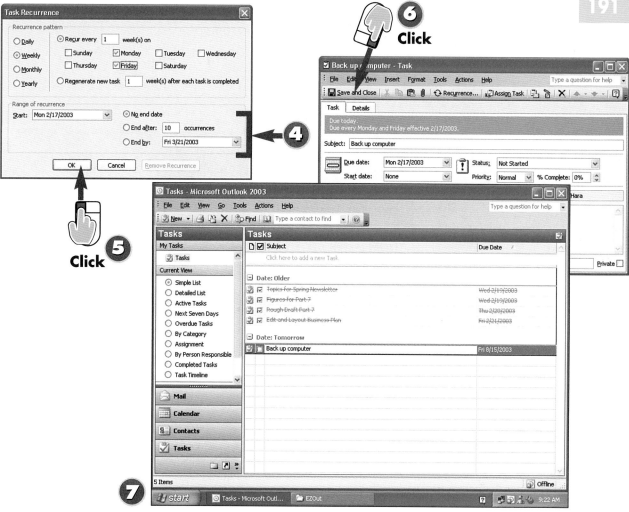

Specify the range of recurrence—that is, over what period of time the recurring appointment will occur.

Click **OK**.

The Tasks window's date and time information lists the recurrence details you entered; click **Save and Close**.

The Tasks list displays a special icon for recurring tasks.

End

Editing a Recurring Task
If you double-click a recurring task in your Tasks list, you are prompted to select whether you want to edit just that specific instance of the task (**Open This Occurrence**) or every instance of it (**Open the Series**) . Make your choice, click **OK**, and then make changes as needed.

Deleting a Recurring Task
To delete a recurring task, click it in the Tasks list and then click Delete. You are then prompted to select whether to delete this and all future recurrences or just this one; make your selection and click **OK**.

Keeping Time and Expense Information for a Task

Start

Click **1**

Click **2**

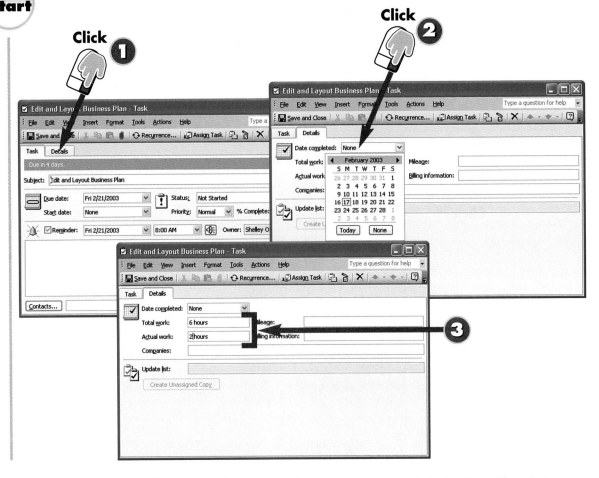

1. After you've created a new task or opened an existing one, click the **Details** tab in the Tasks window.

2. Type the completion date in the **Date Completed** field or click the **down-arrow** button next to the field and choose a date from the minicalendar that appears.

3. Type the total work (the total time you estimate the project will take) and the actual work (the actual time spent on the task) into the respective fields.

INTRODUCTION

Many professionals, such as lawyers and accountants, charge clients an hourly rate. If you bill in a similar way, you can use Outlook to track the amount of time you spend on various tasks. In addition, you can also use Outlook to track expense factors such as mileage.

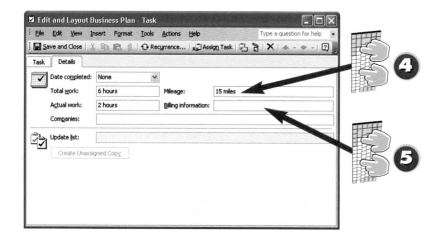

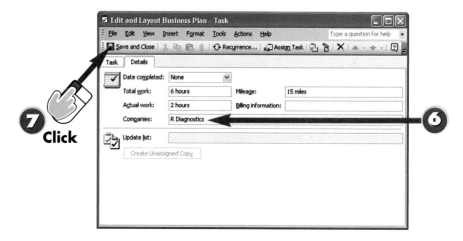

4 Keep track of mileage by typing an amount into the **Mileage** text box.

5 Enter any other miscellaneous billing information into the **Billing Information** field.

6 To keep track of the company or companies associated with the task, type their names into the **Companies** field.

7 Click **Save and Close**.

End

Setting Task Reminders

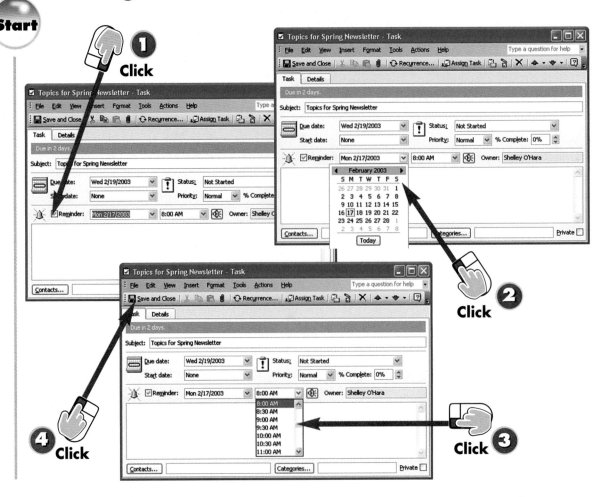

Start

Click ①

Click ②

Click ③

Click ④

① After you've created a new task or opened an existing one, click the **Reminder** check box in the Tasks window.

② Type the date to be reminded in the **Reminder** field or click the **down-arrow** button and choose a date from the minicalendar.

③ Type the time for the reminder to be displayed or click the **down-arrow** button and choose a time.

④ Click **Save and Close**.

End

You can set up Outlook to remind you when a particular task is scheduled or due. Because every task may require different lead times, you can select the date and time for your reminder.

Select Alert Sound

If you really want to get fancy, you can change the sound that is played when an alert is displayed. Click the **Reminder Sound** button and then click the **Browse** button. Change to the drive and folder that contains the sound file you want to play. Select the file and then click **Open**. Click **OK**.

Viewing and Handling Task Reminders

Start

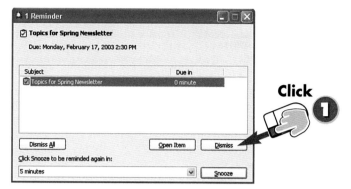

Click 1

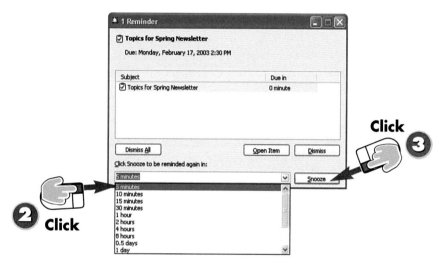

2 Click

Click 3

1. When a Reminder dialog box appears, you'll see the task name and the date and time it's due. To dismiss the reminder (and turn off the alert), click the **Dismiss** button.

2. If you aren't ready to dismiss the reminder and instead want to receive a second reminder after a period of time, select a snooze interval.

3. Click the **Snooze** button. The Reminder dialog box will be redisplayed after the interval you specified in step 2.

End

Opening the Tasks Window
If you want to open the Tasks window to view details about the task or to reschedule it, click **Open Item**. After you've made the desired changes, click **Save and Close**.

Dismissing All Reminders
If you want to dismiss all reminders, click the **Dismiss All** button. You will be asked to confirm that you don't want to be reminded for any scheduled tasks; click **Yes**.

Marking a Task as Complete

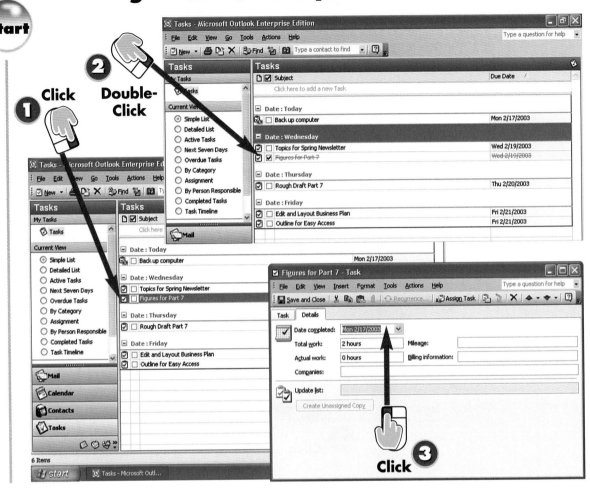

1 In the Tasks list, click the completion check box next to the task.

2 The task is marked completed and formatted in a lighter font and strikethrough. Double-click the task.

3 The Tasks window opens; click the **Details** tab. Notice that Outlook has entered the completion date.

End

The best part of creating a to-do list is marking off those items you complete. Even if you don't get a charge out of checking off the item as complete, consider making the effort anyway; doing so can help you keep track of the date and time when a task was completed.

More Options for Marking a Task Complete

If you prefer, you can mark a task as complete by opening the task and then clicking the **Mark Complete** button, or by opening the **Actions** menu and choosing **Mark Complete**.

Deleting a Task

Start

Click 2

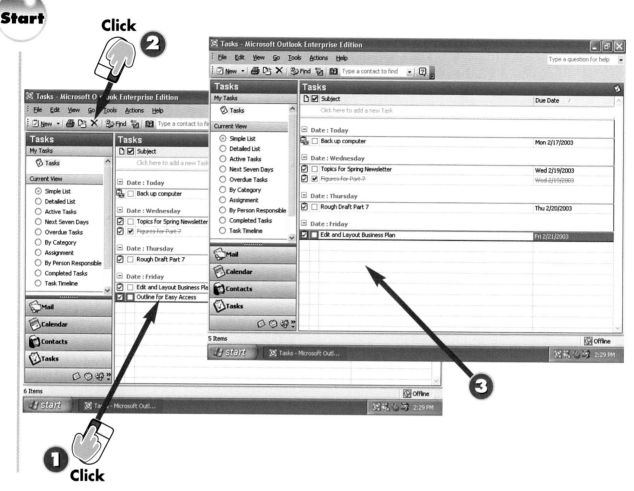

Click 1

1 Click the task in the Tasks list to select it.

2 Click the **Delete** button on the Outlook toolbar.

3 The task is deleted.

End

If you have completed a task, it's best to mark it complete, keeping the item on the Tasks list rather than deleting it. On the other hand, if you add a task by mistake or if you no longer need to complete a task, you might choose to delete it from the list.

Undoing the Deletion

You are not prompted to confirm the deletion, so be sure that you do want the task deleted. If you delete a task by accident and you immediately realize your mistake, you can undo the deletion by opening the **Edit** menu and choosing **Undo**. If you have performed other actions since the deletion, however, issuing the Undo command won't work; you'll have to re-create the task.

Searching for a Task

Start

Click 1

2

Click 3

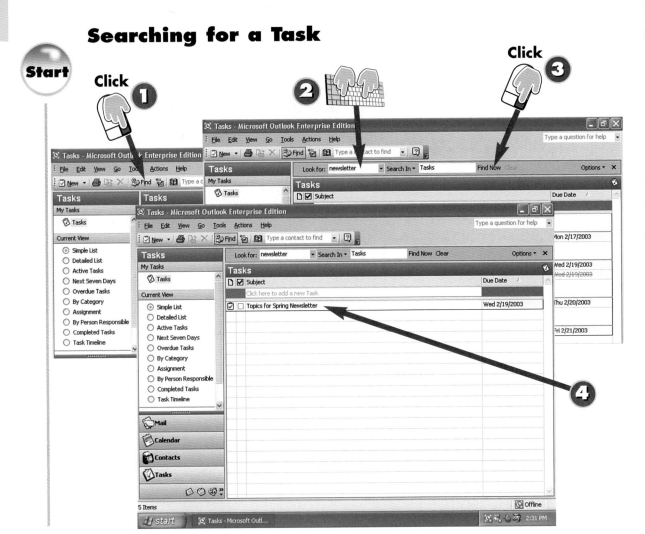

4

---

1 Click the **Find** button on the Outlook window's toolbar.

2 A Find bar appears under the Outlook window's toolbar, displaying the find options. In the **Look For** text box, type a word or phrase used to identify the task.

3 Click the **Find Now** button.

4 Outlook displays matching items in the Tasks list. To close the Find bar, click the **Close** button on the Find bar. The task list now lists all tasks.

End

INTRODUCTION

If you have many tasks scheduled, you may find that scrolling through all the tasks to find the one of interest is time consuming. Instead, you can search for the task. You can also search for a task if you remember only partial details of the task.

Opening an Item
To open a matched item, double-click it in the Search Results window.

Setting Search Options
Change the search options by clicking the **Options** button in the Find bar and then clicking **Advanced Find**. You can select to search based on status, time range, importance, and other task details. Make your choices and click **Find Now**.

Sending a Status Report

Click ① **Click** ②

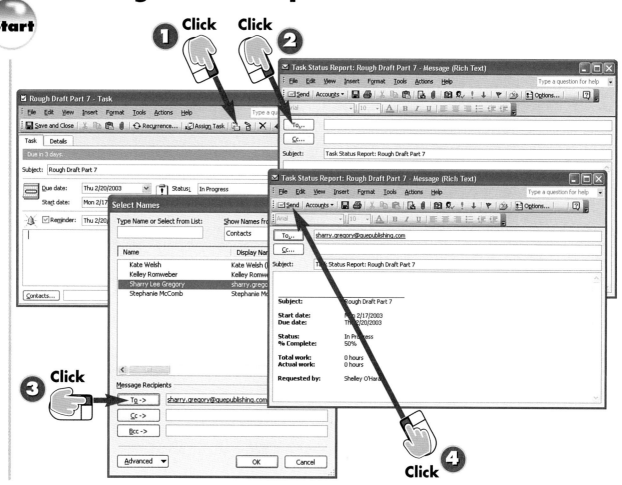

Click ③

Click ④

① After you open the task for which you want to send a report, click the **Send Status Report** button.

② Outlook creates a new mail message with the details of the report. Click the **To** button to select the recipient for the report.

③ Select the person to whom you want to send the status report, and click **To**. The person is added to the message address; click **OK**.

④ The selected name is listed in the mail message. Click the **Send** button in the Message window to send the report.

End

During your work, you may want to inform others of your progress. You can do so by sending a status report. The report will include the task's subject, due date, status, percent complete, total work estimated for the project, actual work, and your name.

Multiple Copies

You can select multiple contacts by selecting each contact and then clicking **To**. You can also send a carbon copy by selecting their names and then clicking **Cc**.

No Overall Report

Outlook does not provide an overall status report on all your tasks. You can, though, view a task timeline by selecting this option under Current View in the task pane.

Setting Up a Tasks List for Printing

Start

Click

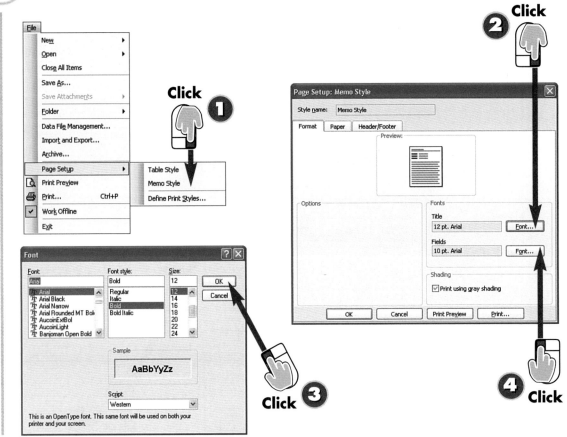

Click

Click

Click

1. Open the **File** menu, choose **Page Setup**, and in the submenu that appears, select the style you want to modify (**Table Style** or **Memo Style**).

2. The Page Setup dialog box opens, displaying the page options for that style. To change the font for the page title, click the **Font** button next to **Title** field.

3. The Font dialog box opens. Select a font, style, and size for the title, and click **OK**.

4. Back in the Page Setup dialog box, change the font for the fields by clicking the **Font** button to the right of the **Fields** entry; repeat step 3 to assign the desired fonts.

INTRODUCTION

There may be times when you want to print your Tasks list. Before you print, however, you must use Outlook's Page Setup options to specify how the printout will look. You can select from two print styles: memo and table. Each style also has various options, such as the orientation of the page, the margins, and the font, which you can change.

TIP

Understanding the Options
The Page Setup options vary depending on the selected printout style. If you are unsure about an option, right-click it and select **What's This?** to view a brief description.

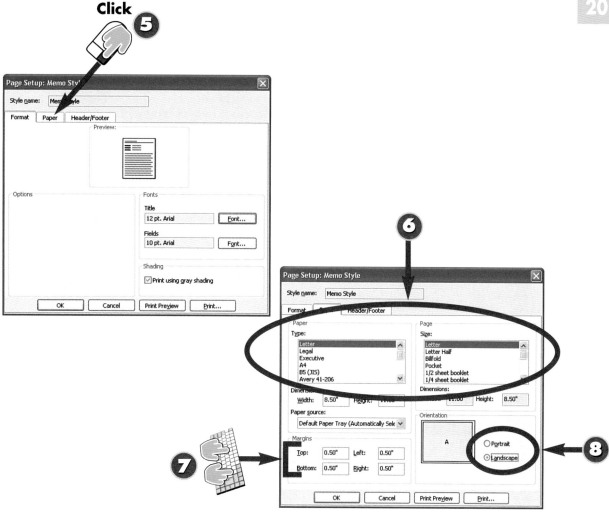

Click 5

6

7

8

---

5 To print the Tasks list on special paper or to change the orientation to better suit the data, click the **Paper** tab in the Page Setup dialog box.

6 Using the **Type** and **Size** lists, select from any number of available paper types and sizes.

7 To change the margins, type new values in the **Top**, **Bottom**, **Left**, or **Right** fields.

8 To change the page's orientation, click the **Landscape** or **Portrait** option button. When you're finished, click **OK**; you're now ready to preview and print the Tasks list.

End

Adding a Header or Footer
You can add a header or a footer to the printout using the Page Setup dialog box's Header/Footer tab. Specify where the text should appear (at the left margin, centered, or at the right margin) and type the text. You can also, if you want, use the handy buttons to insert common header and footer items such as page numbers or dates.

Previewing and Printing
You can preview or print the Tasks list directly from the Page Setup dialog box by clicking the **Print Preview** or **Print** button.

Previewing a Tasks List

Start

Click 3

2

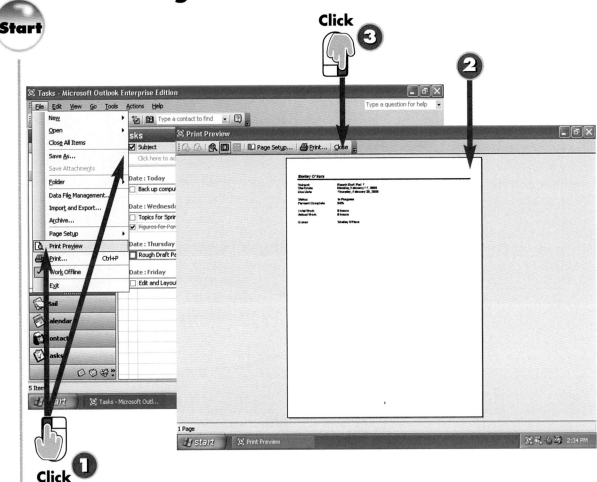

Click 1

1 Open the **File** menu and choose **Print Preview**.

2 A preview of the Tasks list printout appears.

3 When you are finished previewing the printout, click the **Close** button.

End

Before you print your Tasks list, you may want to preview the printout. If the preview doesn't match your expectations, you can make adjustments as needed.

Using the Preview Toolbar
You can use the buttons in the Preview toolbar to zoom in, display multiple pages, access the Page Setup dialog box, or print. Simply click the appropriate button.

Printing from the Print Preview Window
You can print directly from Print Preview by clicking the **Print** button at the top of the window.

Printing a Tasks List

Start

Click

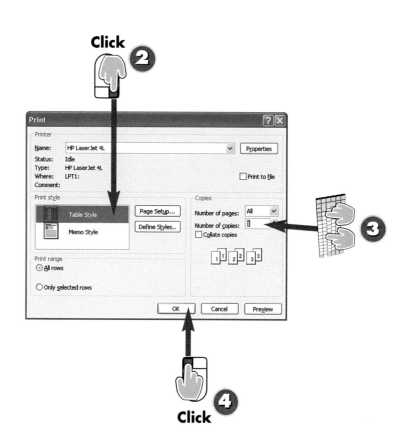

Click

Click

1. Open the **File** menu and choose **Print**.

2. The Print dialog box opens. In the **Print Style** area, select the style you prefer.

3. In the **Number of Copies** field, type the number of copies you want to print.

4. Click **OK** to print your Tasks list.

End

INTRODUCTION

If you need a hard copy of your Tasks list—for example, to use when you are away from your computer or to pass out to participants in a group project—you can print it. Outlook provides two handy task print layouts.

TIP

Print Options
For Table style, you can select the print range—all rows or only selected rows. For Memo style, you can select to start each item on its own page and/or print any attached files.

TIP

Using Print Shortcuts
If you prefer using Outlook's toolbars to its menus, click the **Print** button to open the Print dialog box. Alternatively, press **Ctrl+P**.

Setting Task Options

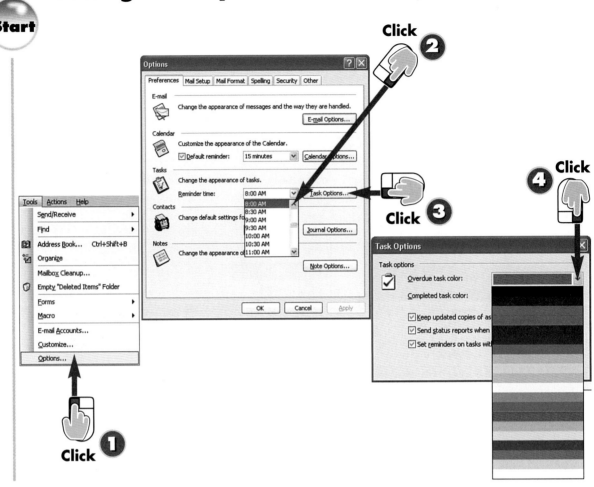

1 Open the **Tools** menu and choose **Options**.

2 The Options dialog box opens with the Preferences tab displayed. To change the
default reminder lead time, click the **down-arrow** button next to **Reminder Time**
field and choose a new lead time.

3 To make other changes, click the **Task Options** button.

4 To change the default color for overdue tasks and/or completed tasks, click the
down-arrow button next to the field and choose a color.

If you like, you can customize
what color is used for overdue
and completed tasks, whether
reminders are set, and other
options.

Getting Help on Options
If you are unsure what a particular option does, right-click the
option and select **What's This?**
to view a brief description.

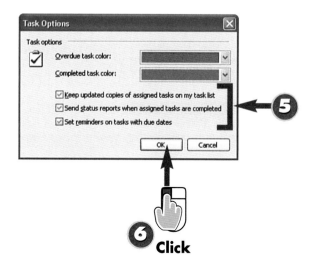

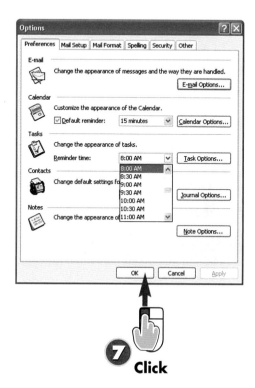

6 Click

7 Click

5 To disable any task options, such as whether status reports are sent, uncheck the appropriate check box.

6 Click **OK**.

7 Back in the Options dialog box, click **OK** to close it.

End

Understanding Default Options
By default, Outlook keeps a list of any assigned tasks, sends status reports when assigned tasks are complete, and sets a reminder for any task for which you enter a due date. You should set these defaults, however, to match your work style. You can always override these options for individual tasks.

Viewing the Notes Window

Start

Click 2

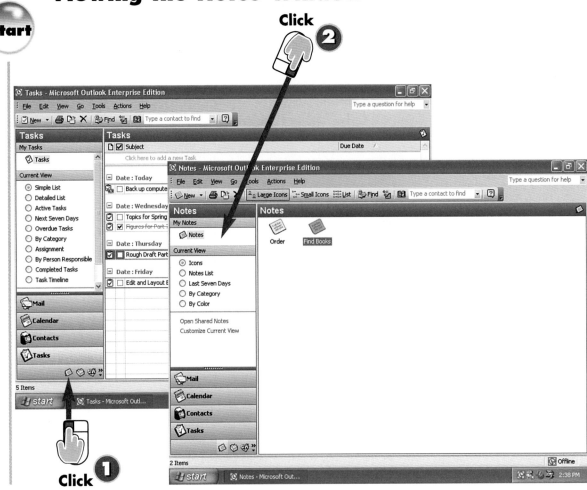

Click 1

1 Click the **Notes** icon in the Outlook Button Bar.

2 The Notes window opens, with the task pane listing the various Notes views.

End

Another feature included with Outlook is the Notes feature. You can use the Notes feature to type little reminders to yourself—reminders that don't fit within the scope of any of the other features (mail messages, appointments, tasks, and so on).

Modifying the Outlook Bar

By default, Notes is displayed as an icon in the Outlook Button bar. You can, however, change how features are displayed in the Outlook Bar (that is, as an icon or a button). See "Customizing the Button Bar" in Part 1, "Getting Acquainted with Outlook 2003," for more information.

Creating a Note

Start

Click **1**

2

Click **3**

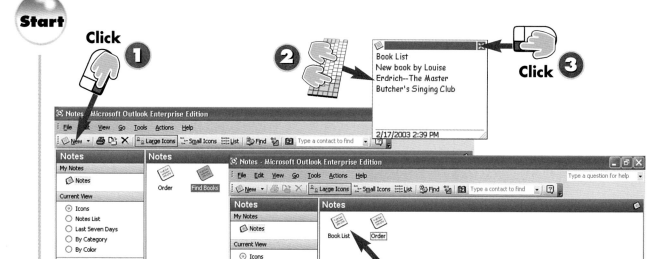

4

1. While in Notes view, click the **New** button on the Outlook toolbar.

2. A small Notes window opens, featuring the current date and time at the bottom. Click anywhere in the window and type your note.

3. Click the **Close** button in the upper-right corner of the small Notes window.

4. The note is added to the Notes area.

End

INTRODUCTION

For information that doesn't fit neatly into a category, you can use Notes. For example, you may want to jot down ideas you have for a new proposal or product, or you might want to make note of a book or article of interest.

Using a Heading
Outlook uses the first line of the note as the note's heading. It's a good practice to type a one-line heading for each note so that you can easily identify its contents from the Notes list.

Changing Note Options
You can set the default Notes options from the Options dialog box. To do so, open the **Tools** menu and choose **Options**. Click the **Note Options** button to set the default note color, text size, and font.

Opening and Editing an Existing Note

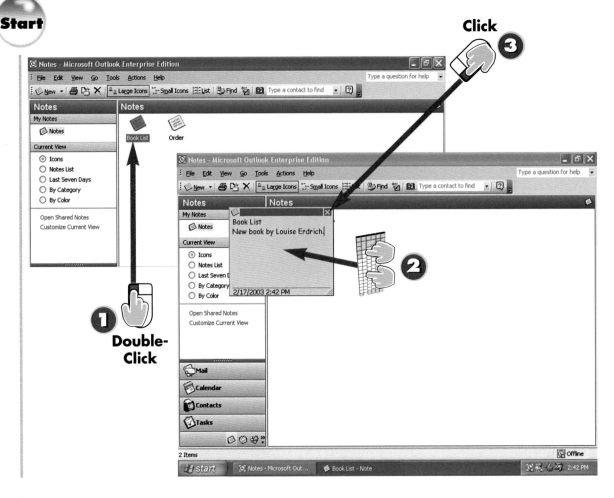

Start

Click

Double-Click

1. Double-click the note you want to view or edit.

2. The note opens. View the note and make changes to it as needed.

3. When you are finished editing the note, click its **Close** button. The note is updated.

End

Of course, the entire point of using Notes is to enable you to view the items you've jotted down at any time, either to review the information or to change it in some way.

Using the Shortcut Menu to Open Notes

You can right-click a note in the Notes list and then click **Open** to open the note.

Color Coding Notes

Start

Click **1**

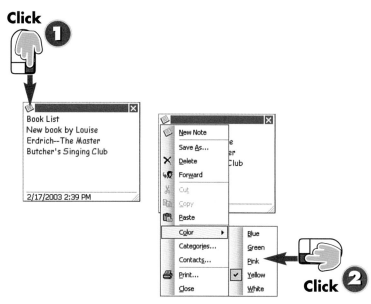

Click **2**

Click **3**

1 After you create or open the note you want to color code, click the **Notes** menu.

2 Click **Color** and then select the desired color from the list.

3 The note is formatted with the selected color; click the **Close** button to close the note.

End

The simplest way to keep your notes organized is to code them so that they are categorized by color. You can then easily view all notes for a particular category—that is, those assigned a particular color.

Using Other Notes Commands

You can use other commands from the Notes menu to save, delete, forward, or print the open note.

Color Coding from the List

You don't have to open a note to color code it; instead, you can assign colors from within the main Notes window. Simply right-click the note you want to change, click **Color**, and select the color you want.

Changing How Notes Are Viewed

Start

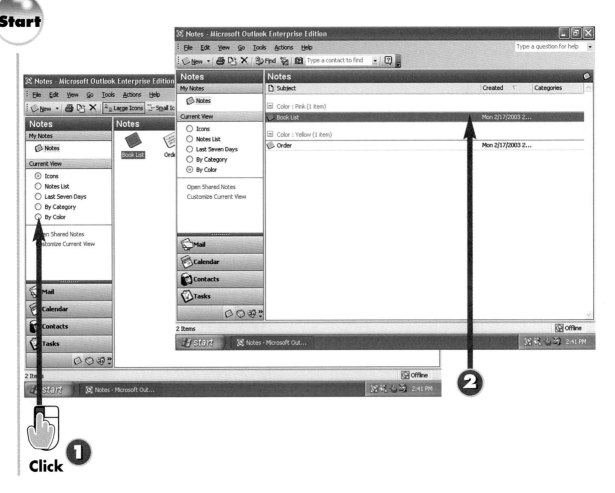

Click

1 The default view for notes is Icons. To change views, click the view you want in the task pane. For example, to view the notes by color, click **By Color**.

2 Outlook uses this view to display the notes.

End

Expanding and Collapsing Items

If the notes are grouped (by date, color, or category), Outlook displays a heading for each note category. You can expand the heading to display the associated notes by clicking the plus sign (+) next to the heading. To collapse or hide the items, click the minus sign (–) next to the heading.

Assigning a Category to a Note

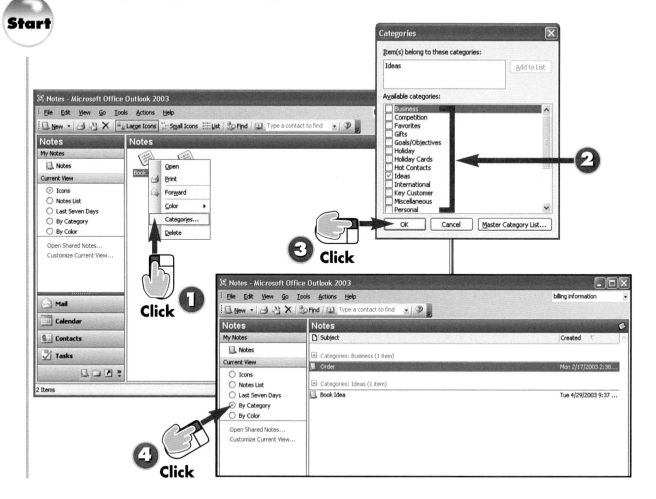

1. Right-click the note to which you want to assign a category and click **Categories**.

2. The Categories dialog box opens, displaying a list of available categories. Mark the check box next to any categories you want to assign to the note.

3. Click **OK**.

4. You won't notice a difference in the note itself, but you can choose to display notes by category, as shown here. To do so, click **By Category** in the task pane.

INTRODUCTION

If you use lots of notes, color-coding them may not be an effective way to keep them organized. Instead, you can assign each a category (such as personal or business). You can then easily view all notes by category, allowing you to keep your notes organized.

Deleting a Note

Start

Click 2

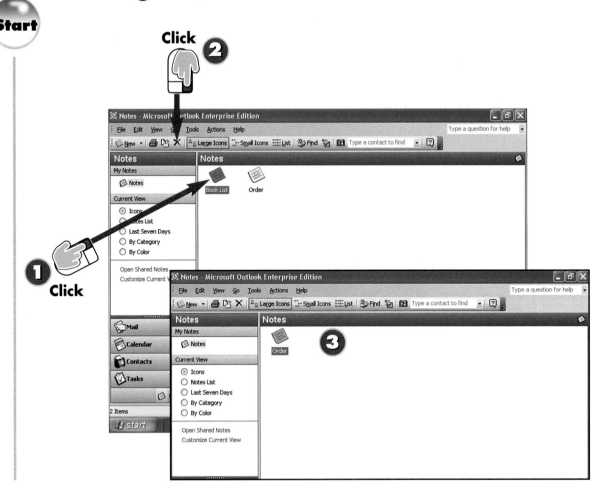

Click 1

1 Click the note you want to delete to select it.

2 Click the **Delete** button on Outlook's toolbar.

3 The note is deleted.

End

To keep your notes organized, you may want to delete any notes that are no longer valid or needed. Note that you are not prompted to confirm the deletion of a note.

Deleting with the Menu or Keyboard

If you prefer, you can right-click the note and select the **Delete** command. Alternatively, you can click the note in the main Notes window to select it and press the **Delete** key on your keyboard.

TIP

Printing a Note

Start

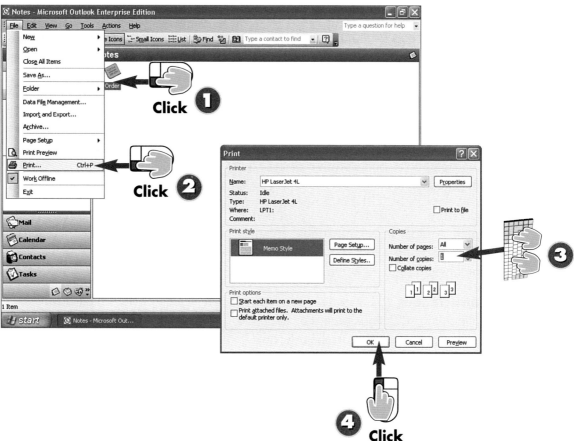

Click ①

Click ②

③

④ Click

① Click the note you want to print to select it.

② Open the **File** menu and choose **Print**.

③ The Print dialog box opens. In the **Number of Copies** field, type the number of copies you want to print.

④ Click **OK**. The note is printed.

End

If you want to print a copy of your note, you can do so. Outlook uses a simple memo style for notes.

Using Print Shortcuts
If you want a quick printout using the default print options, click the note to select it and then click the **Print** button in the Outlook toolbar. Alternatively, right-click the note and choose the **Print** command from the menu that appears.

A

Address Book   An Outlook feature that lets you store address information (including email addresses, notes, and other data) for individuals.

appointment   An activity that you schedule using Calendar. You can enter the date, time, and duration of the appointment.

archive   A file that stores past items such as older email messages, calendars, to-do lists, and so on. You open archived files to view the contents.

attachment   A document that you attach to an Outlook item. For example, you might attach a worksheet to an email message, and send the message and the file to a co-worker.

AutoArchive   An email feature that automatically stores and then removes copies of older messages from your email folders. You can control the settings for whether and when AutoArchive occurs.

AutoSignature   An email feature that lets you quickly add your name and title or other contact information (such as phone or address) to the end of an email.

B–C

Bcc   Stands for "blind carbon copy." You can send a blind carbon copy email to a recipient; that person (or persons) will not be listed on the recipient list but will receive the message.

Calendar   An Outlook feature that enables you to schedule appointments, meetings, and events. You can view the Calendar by day, week, month, or year.

category   A way to group similar items together, such as contacts. You can assign categories to messages, contacts, tasks, and other Outlook items.

Cc   Stands for "carbon copy." You can send a carbon copy email to a recipient; that person will receive a copy of the message.

contact   A record of a person and that person's contact information, including his or her email address, phone number, street address, and other personal details that you choose to note.

D

Deleted Items   An Outlook folder that stores items that you have deleted. You can open this folder to retrieve items, such as email messages, that were deleted by mistake.

distribution list   A group of email recipients. If you frequently send emails to a particular group of people, you can add those people to a distribution list. Then, when you want to send a message to that group, rather than selecting each individual as a recipient, you select that distribution list. The message is sent to all individuals in the distribution list.

draft   A message you have created but are not yet ready to send. You can save the message (in the Drafts folder) and send it later.

Drafts   An Outlook folder that stores messages you have created but not yet sent. If you don't complete a message, you can save it in the Drafts folder, go back later and finish it, and then send the message.

E-F

email   An efficient, inexpensive, quick way of communicating using the Internet. You can use an email program, such as Outlook, to create and send email messages.

email address   The string of characters that identifies someone's email name and provider. The address usually follows this format: **sohara@quepublishing.com**. The first part is the username; the second part is the mail-provider name. The two parts are separated with an @ sign.

event   Something you schedule using the Calendar feature of Outlook. An event may be an appointment, a meeting, or something similar.

Find bar   The bar that appears when you want to search for an item such as a message in your email folders or an event in your Calendar.

flag   A way to mark an item. For instance, you can flag an email message that requires some follow-up action.

folder   In Outlook, the place where email messages are stored. You have folders for messages you have received (Inbox), messages you have sent (Sent Items), messages you have Deleted (Deleted Items), as well as several others. Outlook, like Windows XP, uses folders for storing files and documents.

forward   To send a message along to someone else. For instance, jokes are often forwarded to share with others.

G-I

hyperlink   A Web address typed in the proper format. You can click the address to go to that Web site. See also *Web address*.

IM   See *Instant Messaging (IM)*.

Inbox   An Outlook folder that stores messages that you have received.

Instant Messaging (IM)   An Outlook feature that lets you type text and send it immediately to another individual who is online. You can have a live conversation by typing comments back and forth.

Internet   A network of networks, the Internet enables you to send and receive email. It also enables you to view and access information on the Web.

Internet Explorer   The Internet browser program included with Windows XP and commonly used to view Web pages. You can use the Web toolbar in Outlook to open Internet Explorer and display a Web page.

Internet service provider (ISP)
The company that you use for your Internet connection. You connect to your ISP, and then through that network access Web sites and send and receive email messages.

ISP   See *Internet service provider.*

J–M

journal   A notation of activities associated with a contact—for example, calls, letters, email messages, faxes, and so on.

junk mail   Unsolicited mail. Just as you probably frequently receive junk mail sent via the post, you can also receive junk mail via email. This type of junk email is called *spam.*

link   See *hyperlink.*

mailing list   See **distribution list**.

mail provider   The company that provides your email service. Usually your ISP provides both Internet access and email, although you can sign up for just email accounts with services such as Hotmail.

mail server   The network computer that stores your email messages. When you go online, you download the messages from that computer to your computer. When you set up a mail account in Outlook, you need to enter the server names for both incoming and outgoing mail.

meeting   An activity that you can schedule with Calendar. You send out email invitations to the meeting; recipients then reply to your invitation.

menu   A list of choices or commands for performing tasks within a program. The main menu names are listed in the menu bar. You can display the commands within the menu bar by clicking the menu name.

message   The medium through which you communicate in email. You compose and then send and receive email messages.

modem   To access the Internet, you need a hardware device called a modem. Your modem is connected to your computer, as well as to your Internet service (usually through a phone line or cable).

N–O

Notes   An Outlook component that enables you to type reminder notes.

Outbox   The Outlook folder that stores messages you have created and that are waiting to be sent. You can set up Outlook to send messages immediately, or you can create messages, store them in the Outbox, and then send them manually.

Outlook bar   The left pane of the Outlook window. The top area, often called the *task pane*, lists options for the selected component. The bottom area, called the *button bar*, includes buttons and icons for each of the Outlook components. You can switch to another component by clicking the button or icon in the button bar.

Outlook Express   A pared-down version of Outlook that comes with Windows. It is similar to Outlook but does not include as many features.

Outlook Today   The default view of Outlook that shows an overview of tasks, scheduled events, and messages.

P-R

POP server   The technical name for the incoming mail server. You enter the name of this server when setting up a mail account; the specific name is given to you by your mail provider.

Preview pane   An area of the Outlook window that can be used to display a preview of the selected item. For instance, if you are viewing email messages, the Preview pane displays as much of the selected message as will fit in that pane. You can turn the Preview pane on or off.

reminder   A pop-up window that appears and a sound that plays at the interval you set before an event is scheduled. This reminder helps, well, remind you of your appointments, meetings, and such.

rule   An email feature you can set up to specify how Outlook handles certain messages. For example, you can create a rule that instructs Outlook to place messages from a particular sender in a special folder.

S

Sent Items   An Outlook folder that stores copies of email messages that you have sent.

signature   See *AutoSignature*.

SMTP server   The technical name for the outgoing mail server. You enter the name of this server when setting up a mail account; the specific name is given to you by your mail provider.

stationery   A predesigned email format with graphical elements, such as colors or font changes. You can use stationery to create and send new email messages.

status bar   The bottom bar of the Outlook window. The status bar displays information such as whether you are online.

status report   An element used to track the progress of any scheduled tasks. You can send status reports that show the total time, actual time, progress, and other task details.

subject   One of the header lines for an email message. The subject line helps the recipient identify the contents of the message.

T

Tasks   An Outlook feature that enables you to create a to-do list. You can then track the progress, time, and completion date for each task in the list.

Task pane   The top part of the Outlook Bar. The Task pane displays options related to the selected component. For instance, if you select Tasks, you see the various options for viewing your tasks list.

toolbar   A row of buttons that provide shortcuts to commonly used commands. You can select which toolbars are displayed in Outlook.

U–V

URL   Stands for Uniform Resource Locator. The technical term for a Web address.

vCard   Stands for "Virtual Card." A vCard is a standard format for business cards. You can attach your business information in this format to messages you send.

view   How information is displayed onscreen. Each of the Outlook features has several views in which you can work. For instance, in Calendar, you can work in day view, week view, or month view.

W–Z

Web address   The string of characters that identifies a particular Web site. A Web address usually follows this format: **http://www.quepublishing.com**. **http** stands for Hypertext Transfer Protocol; you can skip this part when typing an address. **www** stands for World Wide Web, which anymore is synonymous with the Internet. The next part is the site name, followed by a period and then the extension. The extension indicates the type of site; common extensions include **gov** for government, **org** for organization, **com** for commercial, and **net** for network.